FATIMA

THE APPARITION THAT CHANGED THE WORLD

FATIMA

THE APPARITION THAT CHANGED THE WORLD

JEAN M. HEIMANN

TAN Books
Charlotte, North Carolina

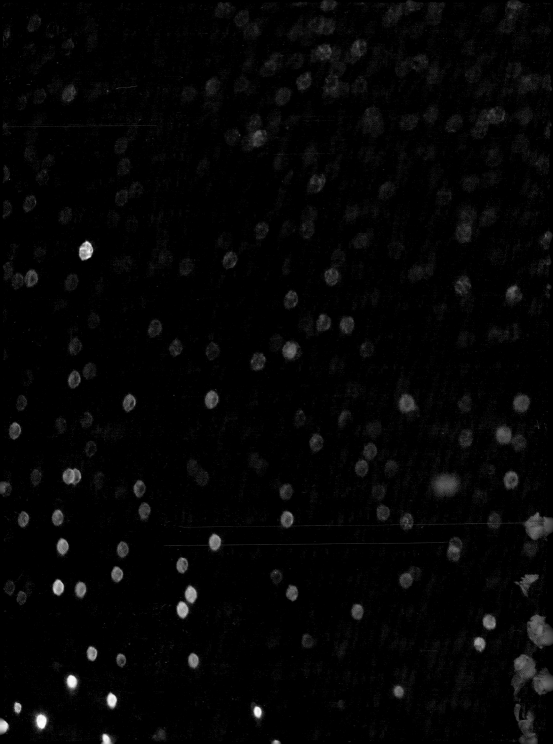

Cover and interior design by Caroline Kiser.

ISBN: 978-1-5051-0953-5

Published in the United States by
TAN Books
PO Box 410487
Charlotte, NC 28241
www.TANBooks.com

Printed and bound in the United States of America

Table of Contents

Timeline

1916

The three shepherd children of Fatima—Lucia dos Santos and her two cousins, Francisco and Jacinta Marto—are visited three times by the Angel of Peace.

1917—May 13

Our Lady appears to the three children at the Cova da Iria and asks that they return for five more months in succession, on the thirteenth day, at the same hour.

June 13

Our Lady tells the children that God wants to establish in the world devotion to the Immaculate Heart of Mary. About seventy people come to the Cova da Iria to witness the apparition.

July 13

Our Lady shows the children a vision of hell and tells them that she will return at a later date to ask for the consecration of Russia to her Immaculate Heart and the Communion of Reparation on the First Saturdays. She tells the children three secrets (also referred to as a secret with three parts) and promises to prove her appearances with a miracle on October 13, 1917. About four thousand people come to witness the apparition.

August 13

The children are kidnapped by the mayor of Ourém and miss their appointed meeting with Our Lady. About eighteen thousand people come to the Cova and many witness mystical phenomena indicating Our Lady's presence.

August 19

Our Lady visits the children in nearby Valinhos and again prophesizes the working of a miracle in October while telling the children to pray and make sacrifices for sinners.

September 13

Our Lady tells the children that Our Lord will come in October, as well as Our Lady of Sorrows and Our Lady of Mount Carmel. Also, St. Joseph will appear with the Child Jesus in order to bless the world. About thirty thousand people come to the Cova, and, again, many witness mystical phenomena representing Our Lady's presence.

October 13

Our Lady announces, "People must amend their lives and ask pardon for their sins. They must not offend Our Lord any more for He is already too much offended." She tells us to continue to pray the Rosary every day. More than one hundred thousand people witness the Miracle of the Sun.

1919–April 4

Francisco dies in Aljustrel at age eleven during an influenza epidemic.

1920–February 20

Jacinta dies in Lisbon at age ten of complications from influenza.

1925–December 10

Our Lady, with the Child Jesus by her side, appears to Lucia in her room at the convent of the Sisters of St. Dorothy in Pontevedra, Spain. Our Lady requests the First Five Saturdays devotion in reparation to her Immaculate Heart.

1929–June 13

Our Lady of Fatima appears to Sister Lucia at Tuy, Spain, in the visible presence of the Holy Trinity and asks for the consecration of Russia to her Immaculate Heart.

1930–May 29–30

Sister Lucia has a mystical experience while speaking with Our Lord in the chapel at Tuy, Spain. He reveals five kinds of blasphemies and offenses spoken against the Immaculate Heart of Mary.

October 13

The bishop of Fatima declares the supernatural origin of the Fatima apparitions worthy of acceptance.

1938–January

Sister Lucia views the extraordinary lights that illuminate the skies of Europe on the night of January 25–26, 1938, during the hours of 8:45 p.m. to 1:15 a.m., as "the great sign"—the unknown light that Our Lady of Fatima predicted and which would serve as a signal that war was near.

1939–September 1

World War II begins and lasts until September 2, 1945. Marked by the death of civilians on a monumental scale—including the Holocaust and the only use of nuclear weapons in warfare—it was the deadliest conflict in human history, resulting in more than seventy million fatalities.

1940–December 2

Sister Lucia writes a letter to Pius XII asking the Holy Father for "blessing and extending this devotion [to the Immaculate Heart of Mary] to the whole world and for the consecration of the world to the Immaculate Heart of Mary, with special mention of Russia."

1942–OCTOBER 31 AND DECEMBER 8

Pope Pius XII consecrates the Church and the human race to the Immaculate Heart of Mary. However, he does not specifically consecrate Russia to her Immaculate Heart.

MAY 4

Pope Pius XII institutes the feast of the Immaculate Heart of Mary.

1946–MAY 13

Pope Pius XII crowns the image of Our Lady of Fatima and proclaims her "Queen of the World."

1952–JULY 7

Pope Pius XII consecrates the Russian people to the Immaculate Heart.

1962–DECEMBER 13

Pope John XXIII institutes the feast of Our Lady of the Rosary in honor of Our Lady of Fatima.

1964–NOVEMBER 21

Pope Paul VI renews Pius XII's consecration of Russia to the Immaculate Heart of Mary, speaking to the Fathers of the Second Vatican Council.

1981–MAY 13

Pope John Paul II is shot and seriously wounded by an assassin.

1982–MARCH 21

Sister Lucia informs the papal nuncio of the requirements for a valid consecration of Russia according to the request of Our Lady of Fatima.

MAY 13

Pope John Paul II makes his first pilgrimage to Fatima to pray in thanksgiving for his surviving the attempted assassination on May 13, 1981. He consecrates the world, but not Russia, at Fatima. The Catholic bishops of the world do not participate.

1984–MARCH 25

Pope John Paul II, before 250,000 people in Rome, and in union with the bishops throughout the world, consecrates the world to the Immaculate Heart of Mary. Immediately after he pronounces the words of consecration, he departs from his prepared text and prays, "Enlighten especially the peoples of which You Yourself are awaiting our consecration and confiding." Sister Lucia would later confirm that this consecration was acceptable.

1989–NOVEMBER 9

The fall of the Berlin Wall.

1991–MAY 12 AND 13

Pope John Paul II makes his second pilgrimage to Fatima.

DECEMBER 26

The USSR is dissolved. The Cold War ends, and religious freedom is returned to the Russian people.

2000–MAY 13

Pope John Paul II makes his third pilgrimage to Fatima, and the visionaries Jacinta and Francisco Marto are beatified.

JUNE 26

The Vatican publishes the third part of the secret of Fatima.

2005–FEBRUARY 13

Sister Lucia of Fatima dies in the Carmelite convent of St. Teresa in Coimbra less than two months short of her ninety-eighth birthday.

April 2

Death of Pope St. John Paul II on a First Saturday and the Vigil of Divine Mercy Sunday.

2007–May 13

Pope Benedict XVI invokes Our Lady of Fatima on the ninetieth anniversary of the apparitions, stating, "In a special way we entrust to Mary those people and nations that are in particular need, confident that she will not fail to heed the prayers we make to her with filial devotion."

February 14

Benedict XVI lifts the normal five-year waiting period to begin Sister Lucia's canonization process.

April 30

The bishop of Coimbra opens the cause of beatification of Sister Maria Lucia of Jesus and the Immaculate Heart.

October 13

Pope Francis has the original statue of Our Lady of Fatima with the assassin's bullet in the crown brought to St. Peter's Square and consecrates the world to the Immaculate Heart.

Foreword

One hundred years ago we were all given a mission to work tirelessly for the conversion of sinners and to make reparation for sin. The world, which was in turmoil, was given a choice: continue on the course of confusion and destruction or follow a course of sanity and reparation. Many understood this and took up the mission of returning both themselves and the world to a way of life in accord with the laws of God. Many more, however, did not, and the bloody history of the prior century stands as a testimony to this.

On May 13, 1917, Our Lady appeared to Lucia dos Santos and Francisco and Jacinta Marto. She presented to them a message of both warning and hope. It then became clear why they had received three visits from the Angel of Peace the year before. It was to prepare them for the task that would be set before them during the coming months, a task to bring to a wounded world a solution from Almighty God.

Fatima: The Apparition That Changed The World by Jean M. Heimann describes with great accuracy the mission of the Queen of Heaven as she continues to care for her children. Beautifully illustrated, this book brings us through the history of the apparitions of Our Lady and puts the message into perspective. It also presents the significance of Fatima going forward.

With a mother's love, Our Lady explained the reality that war is a punishment for sin and showed the children a vision of hell, illustrating that sin has consequences both in the here and now and eternally. She then presented a peace plan from heaven. Prayer, especially the Rosary, is the key to attaining the great promises that she made to the world and the key to avoiding the terrible things of which she warned us.

We look at the world today and think that we have not done what she asked. To a great extent this is true, but we must also look at the prayers and good works of many who did, in fact, do as she requested. Think of how much worse things could be if it were not for the many who followed her pleadings, lived just lives, and made reparation for sin. I truly believe that our organization, The World Apostolate of Fatima, has played a major role in shaping world events and helping the world avoid an even worse fate. Numerous Rosaries and many hours of Eucharistic adoration were offered, and more terrible things that might have occurred were avoided.

"Lord, if there are fifty just people, will you spare the city for their sake," Abraham pleaded for the people of Sodom (see Gn 18: 24–33). Our Lord said that he would. As Abraham persisted, asking if his mercy would extend if there were only forty, then thirty, and so on down to ten, the Good Lord agreed. His mercy endures. He wants to extend it to us, but we must turn to him and ask for it. Our Lady at Fatima told us how to ask and what to do.

We may seem more and more like a minority in this world today. Even many Catholics fail to see the importance of prayer and of living faithfully according to the laws of the Church. We, however, understand that we are called to pray, live faithfully, and make reparation for those who don't understand. At the wedding feast of Cana, Mary told the wine steward, "Do whatever he tells you." They did, and Our Lord began his public ministry at that moment. We, like good stewards of God's revelation, must continue to heed our Blessed Mother as she points us to hear and follow her Son.

We must pray constantly that people will take up the call to holiness, but we can never let the lack of response by others deter us in our duty to fulfill the promise that we have made to Our Lady, to work tirelessly for the salvation of souls. This is our mission. It is why the "Blue Army" was founded and why we will not rest until we are called home. The triumph of the Immaculate Heart will come about when we have earned it by our prayers and sacrifices. Working for this is our duty and bringing others to do the same is our goal going forward. If you are not part of our organization, we invite you to join us in this most noble mission, coming as it does directly from the Mother of God.

Fatima: The Apparition That Changed The World, not only presents the history of the apparitions of Our Lady of Fatima, but addresses what the message is today. The hundredth anniversary of Our Lady's appearances is not only a time for reflection or looking back. It is a time to look ahead and to redouble our efforts in bringing people to live the Fatima message. We must all be dedicated to this cause. Fatima is about more than predictions and warnings. If we look only to these things, it is nothing more than a series of historical occurrences. Fatima gives us a prescription for life. Where there is life there is hope, and it is not too late to turn to God and respond generously to his entreaties to follow him. Our Lady pleads with us to do so.

Our Lady of Fatima, pray for us.

—David Carollo
Executive Director, World Apostolate
of Fatima USA, *Our Lady's Blue Army*

Prelude

THE PREPARATION BY THE ANGEL

On a brisk spring day in 1916, three children—Lucia dos Santos (age nine) and her cousins, Francisco (age eight) and Jacinta Marto (age six)—were tending their sheep in a pasture near their home in the mountain village of Fatima, Portugal. At noon, it began to drizzle, and they took shelter in a nearby cave. There they ate their lunch and prayed the Rosary. When the rain stopped, they came out to play a game. Suddenly, in the midst of the calm day, a strong gust of wind shook the treetops. When the children looked up, they saw a brilliant crystal clear light moving toward them that transformed into the figure of a dazzling young man dressed in white. He said, "Do not be afraid! I am the Angel of Peace. Pray with me."

Then the angel knelt down and touched his forehead to the ground. He asked the children to repeat the following prayer three times: "My God, I believe, I adore, I trust, and I love You! I ask pardon for those who do not believe, do not adore, do not trust, and do not love You."

The children were deeply moved by the angel's message. Following the apparition, they frequently prostrated themselves, repeating the prayer many times. Lucia realized that this visit was sacred and private. Thus, she asked her cousins to keep the apparition secret.

In the summer of 1916, when the children were playing at the well in the family garden at Arniero, the angel returned a second time and said, "What are you doing? Pray! Pray much! The Hearts of Jesus and Mary have designs upon you. Offer prayers and sacrifices constantly to the Most High."

Lucia asked, "How must we sacrifice?" The angel replied, "Make of everything you can a sacrifice and offer it to God as an act of reparation for the sins by which He is offended and in supplication for the conversion of sinners. You will thus draw down peace upon your country. I am its Guardian Angel, the Angel of Portugal. Above all, accept and bear with submission the suffering which the Lord will send you."

The Angel of Peace visited them a third time in the fall of 1916. This time, he was holding a golden chalice in his left hand with the Eucharistic Host above it. Bright red drops of the precious Blood of Jesus fell from the Host into the chalice. Then, while the Host was suspended in midair, the angel bowed deeply, pressing his forehead to the ground, and asked the children to repeat this prayer three times:

> O Most Holy Trinity—Father, Son and Holy Spirit—I adore Thee profoundly. I offer Thee the most precious Body, Blood, Soul and Divinity of Jesus Christ, present in all the tabernacles of the world, in reparation for the outrages, sacrileges, and indifferences whereby He is offended. And through the infinite merits of His Most Sacred Heart and the Immaculate Heart of Mary, I beg of Thee the conversion of poor sinners.

As the angel gave the Host to Lucia and the Blood to Francisco and Jacinta, he said, "Take and drink the Body and Blood of Jesus Christ, horribly outraged by ungrateful men! Make reparation for their crimes and console your God!"

The angel bowed deeply, recited the prayer to the Holy Trinity three times, and then vanished. The children repeated the prayer three times and were in such a state of holy ecstasy that they were oblivious to everything around them. They were totally focused on Jesus and the message he was conveying through the Angel of Peace.

The Visionaries of Fatima

Lucia dos Santos

Lucia dos Santos was the oldest of the three visionaries at Fatima. She was the first cousin of the other two, Francisco and Jacinta Marto. Born on March 28, 1907, Lucia was the youngest child of António dos Santos and Maria Rosa of Aljustrel, a hamlet forming part of the remote mountain village of Fatima. Her father was a farmer who owned small portions of land in Montelo, Our Lady of Ortiga, Fatima, Valinhos, Cabeco, Charneca, and Cova da Iria. In her memoirs, Lucia describes her father as a diligent and kind man. He was typical of many of the men of his class. He worked hard, performed his religious obligations, and spent his leisure time in the tavern with his friends.

Her mother, Maria Rosa, was the parent who raised the children, and she did so somewhat strictly. Unlike most peasant women of her day, Maria Rosa was able to read (but never taught her children to do so). Her reading ability enabled her to instruct not only her own children in the catechism but the neighbors' children as well. She also acted as a nurse to her neighbors and cared for those with both minor and serious illnesses.

The family lived out their Catholic faith devoutly. They prayed together each evening, and Maria Rosa read to the children from the Bible or other holy books. Maria's father led the family prayers each evening.

Spiritually mature and gifted for her age, Lucia made her first Holy Communion at the age of six rather than the customary age of ten. She was highly intelligent with an exceptional memory. Her mother reported that she repeated everything she heard "like a parrot." Thus, she learned her catechism very quickly.

On the day before her first Holy Communion, God granted Lucia a special grace regarding her mission in life. After she made her first confession, Lucia went to the altar of Our Lady of the Holy Rosary to pray. There she prayed to Our Lady over and over, "Lord, make me holy, preserve my heart always pure, for you alone." In response, the statue smiled at her, and Our Lady reassured her that she would indeed do so. Lucia's heart was filled with joy and gratitude.

Lucia was a robust and healthy child. Affectionate and loving, she enjoyed caring for the children of others and was resourceful in keeping them busy and entertained. They loved her and always looked forward to her company. Extroverted and lively, Lucia enjoyed singing and dancing at religious festivals and was especially fond of dressing up for these events. Because one of her older sisters was a dressmaker, Lucia wore the most colorful and ornate costumes, and she loved the attention this distinction afforded her.

At the age of seven, Lucia began her work tending the sheep with various boys and girls from the village. At the age of nine, she chose to herd her sheep with her cousins Jacinta and Francisco Marto. She was ten years old when Our Lady first appeared to the children at Fatima.

Francisco Marto

Francisco was born on June 11, 1908. He was the eighth of nine children born to Manuel Marto and Olimpia Jesus dos Santos—the sister of Lucia's father, António dos Santos. And so Francisco was the older brother of Jacinta and the first cousin of Lucia dos Santos. At the time of the apparitions, he was nine years old. In her memoirs, Lucia describes him as being passive and pensive in temperament. In contrast to his vivacious younger sister, Jacinta, he was quiet, easygoing, and almost indifferent. If someone took something belonging to him, he was content to let them keep it. He often let others play the games they preferred and permitted them to win points they had not earned. He was also a contemplative. He enjoyed watching the sun rise and set and routinely went up to the mountaintop to play his flute and sing songs to the Lord. His devotion to private prayer and contemplation increased over time following the apparitions.

Francisco was empathetic and got along well with others. He showed considerable compassion for the sick. He was a congenial young man who smiled often and played with all the other children. He loved animals, especially birds, which he fed daily with crumbs of his own bread. He played with lizards and snakes, feeding them goat's milk.

Jacinta Marto

Jacinta Marto, the youngest of the visionaries, was born on March 11, 1910. She was just seven when Our Lady appeared to the shepherd children. She was the younger sister of Francisco and the first cousin of Lucia dos Santos. Despite her young age, Jacinta gave evidence of a strong character. She exhibited a strong will, a tendency to be assertive, and a stubborn streak. As the youngest child, she had been a bit spoiled and liked doing things her own way. For example, she insisted on playing the games that she enjoyed and selecting the partners she preferred. When she did not get her way, she pouted. At the same time, she was a vivacious, affectionate, and delightful child who loved to dance and sing. She was often viewed as lovable and attractive by others. A sensitive and compassionate child, she wept bitterly when she heard the Passion being read out loud and made up her mind never to cause Jesus suffering again.

The First Two Apparitions

THE FIRST APPARITION—MAY 13, 1917

Approximately one year after the Angel of Peace's initial visit, the shepherd children witnessed their first Marian apparition. On May 13, 1917, Lucia, Francisco, and Jacinta were tending their flocks of sheep in a hollow, the Cova da Iria, which was also known as the Cove of Irene or the Cove of Peace. When they heard the Angelus church bells ring, they knelt down and prayed the Rosary. It was a beautiful sunny day with a clear blue sky. Suddenly a flash of lightning pierced the sky. They thought a storm might be brewing, so they quickly moved their sheep and headed in the direction of home when they spotted another even more striking flash of lightning. There, above a small holm oak tree, was an intense light. Then, in an instant, they saw a lovely lady dressed in white, hovering over the top of the tree.

Lucia described her in this way: "She was more brilliant than the sun, and radiated light more clear and intense than a crystal glass filled with sparkling water when the rays of the burning sun shine through it."

Lucia also stated that the lady appeared to be around seventeen years old, wore a floor-length white veil embroidered with gold trim, and held a rosary of white pearls with a silver cross. The expression on her face was one of slight sorrow.

The lady sensed the apprehension of the children and told them not to be afraid. She reassured them of their safety. She spoke softly to them in a calm voice, and they immediately felt the peace and the presence of Christ's love surround them. They felt comforted by her and responded to her maternal voice with joy and natural curiosity. All three of the children were able to see Our Lady, but only Lucia and Jacinta could hear her. Lucia was the only one of the three who actually conversed with her.

"Where are you from?" Lucia asked.

"I am from heaven," the lady answered.

Lucia queried, "What do you want of me?"

The lady replied, "I have come to ask you to come here for six months in succession, on the thirteenth day, at this same hour. Later on, I will tell you who I am and what I want."

Lucia then asked if each of the children would go to heaven. The lady stated that Lucia and Jacinta would but that Francisco would have to pray many Rosaries. Lucia named two of her friends who had died and inquired whether or not they were in heaven. She learned that one was in heaven, but the other was in purgatory and would be there until the end of time.

The lady then asked the children a crucial question: "Are you willing to offer yourselves to God and bear all the sufferings He wills to send you, as an act of reparation for the sins by which He is offended, and of supplication for the conversion of sinners?"

"Yes, we are willing."

"Then you are going to have much to suffer, but the grace of God will be your comfort."

When she said this, the lady opened up her hands, "communicating to us a light so intense that, as it streamed from her hands, its rays penetrated our hearts and the innermost depths of our souls, making us see ourselves in God, Who was that light, more clearly than we see ourselves in the best of mirrors."

The children then immediately fell to their knees and prayed, "O most Holy Trinity, I adore You! My God, my God, I love You in the most Blessed Sacrament!" After a few minutes, the lady asked them to pray the Rosary every day to obtain peace for the world and an end to the war.

The Second Apparition—June 13, 1917

The second apparition took place on the feast of St. Anthony of Padua, which is a major feast day for the people of Portugal, as St. Anthony is one of the great patrons of that country. Most of us know him as St. Anthony of Padua, but to the Portuguese people, he is known as St. Anthony of Lisbon because that is where he was born. June 13 was a special feast day in the village where the children lived, for the parish church was named for the great wonder-worker. Following the festivities at their parish, about seventy people accompanied the children to the Cova da Iria for their noon meeting with Our Lady.

During the apparition, other than the visionaries, none of those present were able to see Our Lady. However, the others did observe several signs that something extraordinary was happening. The day was hot and sunny as it usually is in Portugal during the month of June, but during the apparition, the sunlight dimmed for no apparent reason and the uppermost branches of the holm oak tree had bent in the shape of an umbrella. Those close to the visionaries heard not only Lucia's voice but also that of a bee buzzing or a whispering sound in response to her voice.

The children knelt under the shade of the holm oak tree and began praying the Rosary. Even the spectators joined in the prayers. When they had finished their prayers, a sudden flash of lightning appeared. Lucia asked Our Lady her usual question, "What do you ask of me?"

Our Lady made three separate requests. First, she requested that the children meet her in the same location on July 13. Second, she asked them once again to pray the Rosary every day. Third, she requested that Lucia learn to read, adding that the reason for this would be revealed later. Eventually Our Lady revealed that she desired Lucia to learn to read in order to spread the message of Fatima to the entire world.

This was to be Lucia's special mission in this life.

Lucia asked Our Lady to heal a sick person. The Virgin Mary told her that the person would be cured within the year if he converted. Lucia also asked the Blessed Mother if she would take her and the other visionaries to heaven. Our Lady replied, "Yes. I will take Jacinta and Francisco soon. But you are to stay here some time longer. Jesus wishes to make use of you to make me known and loved. He wants to establish in the world devotion to my Immaculate Heart."

Then Our Lady opened her hands and radiant rays of light poured out upon the earth. Lucia added, "In front of the palm of Our Lady's right hand was a heart encircled by thorns which pierced it. We understood that this was the Immaculate Heart of Mary, outraged by the sins of humanity, seeking reparation."

LESSONS FROM THE APPARITION

Obedience to the Will of God in Fulfilling Their Mission

Our Lady gave the visionaries the mission to pray and to sacrifice to bring about world peace. In this first apparition, she did not tell them what their sacrifice would be. She simply asked if they were willing to sacrifice. God created all of us with a free will, and when he asks us to perform some special duty or mission for him, we have the ability to choose whether or not we want to do what he asks of us.

At the Annunciation, the Archangel Gabriel first asked the Blessed Virgin Mary if she was willing to be the mother of God. This was God's mission for her, but it was never a task that was imposed on her. It was her decision whether or not she would do God's will. Mary listened to the voice of God and freely submitted her entire being to the plan of God over her life. Through her selfless surrender to his will—her fiat—

Mary immediately began cooperating with the entire work of what Jesus would accomplish. The word *obey* comes from the Latin *obaudire* which means "to hear" or "listen to." It was Mary's faith, humility, and simplicity that allowed her to listen to God and to put his plan into practice. However, Mary did not simply submit to God's will; she longed to fulfill it. When Mary responded, "Let it be done unto me," she did not passively accept the Lord's will but actively and enthusiastically embraced it. Mary was motivated, above all, by love. She lovingly and obediently embraced God's will in her life and made it her own.

In a similar manner, the visionaries at Fatima did not just simply say "yes" to God, but they joyfully and enthusiastically embraced his will. They were first shown their own reflection and their own souls in the light of the reflection of God. They were clearly shown the truth of how God sees them. At that moment, they resembled God in the light because they were made in his image and likeness. They realized how much God loved them and what he had sacrificed for them. They saw God's beauty and love and understood that they had been specifically chosen by him to carry out this special mission on earth. They loved God and fervently desired to please him. Like Mary, and in her presence, the children recognized who they were in the sight of God. In spite of their limitations, they surrendered to him with a willingness to be used as his instruments, with the faith that "nothing will be impossible" with God (Lk 1:37). They joyfully and zealously embraced God's will for their lives and spontaneously fell on their knees and told God how much they loved him. The Angel of Peace prepared them well for the task that lay ahead and they accepted it, relying on the graces that Our Lady had promised.

Reparation

In this apparition, Our Lady mentioned reparation for the first time. Reparation is the repairing or compensating for the offenses committed against God. In justice, but also out of love of God, we need to repair the damage we have done in our relationship with him. Through acts of reparation, we try to compensate for the wrongdoing—the sin that has hurt God and damaged our relationship with him. We may also make reparation for the ways in which others have offended God.

The Rosary

This request by the Mother of God to pray the Rosary was not made for the first time at Fatima. Our Lady has asked us many times in numerous apparitions to do so. She appeared to St. Dominic and Blessed Alan de la Roche in the thirteenth century to initiate the devotion of the Rosary. At that time, Mary taught the Rosary to these two holy men of God to promote the habit of daily prayer among all the faithful, not just those in religious vocations. The Blessed Mother told Alan de la Roche, "When you say your Rosary, the angels rejoice, the Blessed Trinity delights in it, my Son finds joy in it too, and I myself am happier than you can possibly guess. After the Holy Sacrifice of the Mass, there is nothing in the Church that I love as much as the Rosary." When she appeared to them, Our Lady made fifteen promises to those who pray the Rosary.

Numerous saints have also advocated praying the Rosary daily. St. Padre Pio tells us, "The Rosary is the 'weapon' for these times." He adds, "Some people are so foolish that they think they can go through life without the help of the Blessed Mother. Love the Madonna and pray the Rosary, for her Rosary is the weapon against the evils of the world today. All graces given by God pass through the Blessed Mother."

The Fifteen Promises of Our Lady

Made to St. Dominic and Blessed Alan de la Roche

1. To all those who shall recite my Rosary devoutly, I promise my special protection and very great graces.

2. Those who shall persevere in the recitation of my Rosary shall receive some signal grace.

3. The Rosary shall be a very powerful armor against hell; it will destroy vice, deliver from sin, and dispel heresy.

4. The Rosary will make virtue and good works flourish, and will obtain for souls the most abundant divine mercies; it will substitute in hearts love of God for love of the world, and will lift them to the desire of heavenly and eternal things. How many souls shall sanctify themselves by this means!

5. Those who trust themselves to me through the Rosary shall not perish.

6. Those who shall recite my Rosary devoutly, meditating on its mysteries, shall not be overwhelmed by misfortune. The sinner shall be converted; the just shall grow in grace and become worthy of eternal life.

7. Those truly devoted to my Rosary shall not die without the Sacraments of the Church.

8. Those who recite my Rosary shall find during their life and at their death the light of God, the fullness of His graces, and shall share in the merits of the blessed.

9. I shall deliver very promptly from purgatory the souls devoted to my Rosary.

10. The true children of my Rosary shall enjoy great glory in heaven.

11. What you ask through my Rosary, you shall obtain.

12. Those who propagate my Rosary shall be aided by me in all their necessities.

13. I have obtained from my Son that all the members of the Rosary Confraternity shall have for their brethren the saints of heaven during their life and at the hour of death.

14. Those who recite my Rosary faithfully are all my beloved children, the brothers and sisters of Jesus Christ.

15. Devotion to my Rosary is a great sign of predestination.

Throughout history, the recitation of the Rosary has resulted in many miracles. October 7 is the feast of Our Lady of the Rosary. This feast was instituted by Pope St. Pius V in thanksgiving for the great naval victory over the Turks at the battle of Lepanto on that day in the year 1570, a favor due to the recitation of the Rosary. This victory saved Europe from being overrun by the forces of Islam.

In modern times, successive popes have urged the faithful to pray the Rosary. It is a form of contemplative, mental, and vocal prayer, which brings down God's blessing on the Church. It is a biblically inspired prayer that is centered on meditation on the salvific mysteries of Christ in union with Mary, who was so closely associated with her Son in his redeeming activity.

The Rosary is essentially a meditation on the Gospel message. It is scriptural by its very nature. For all who pray it acceptably, it is "a simple method of getting closer to God" (Sister Lucia, *Memoirs*). The correct way of praying the Rosary is to pray it slowly and reverently, from the heart, using each decade to reflect on some aspect of the Joyful, Sorrowful, Luminous, or Glorious Mysteries, such as the fruits of the Mysteries. The Rosary is not a mere rote recitation of prayers but a meditation on the grace of God. Without that contemplative component, we miss the essence, the true vital power of this most popular devotion. Without reflection and meditation on the Mysteries of the Rosary, it would simply be reduced to monotonous repetition. As Pope Paul VI revealed in his apostolic letter *Marialis Cultus*, "Without this [contemplation] the Rosary is a body without a soul, and its recitation is in danger of becoming a mechanical repetition of formulas."

The Third Apparition—
July 13, 1917

The July 13 apparition at Fatima is considered one of the most important apparitions because it was then that Our Lady disclosed the essential meaning of her Fatima message. It was at that time that she imparted many grave warnings but also instilled hope by promising that in the end her "Immaculate Heart would triumph." It was also during this apparition that Our Lady revealed three secrets to the shepherd children.

Lucia asked her usual question, "What do you want of me?"

Our Lady replied, "I want you to come here on the thirteenth of next month and to continue to pray the Rosary every day in honor of Our Lady of the Rosary, in order to obtain peace for the world and the end of the war, for she alone can be of any avail."

Lucia made the following request: "I would like to ask you to tell us who you are and to perform a miracle so everybody will believe that you are appearing to us." Our Lady promised that in October, she would reveal her identity and perform a miracle so that everyone would believe. Lucia then made several requests for conversions and cures. Our Lady recommended the constant recitation of the Rosary for those requests.

Our Lady continued, "Sacrifice yourselves for sinners and say many times, especially when you make a sacrifice, 'O Jesus, this is for love of Thee, for the conversion of sinners, and in reparation for the sins committed against the Immaculate Heart of Mary.'" As she spoke these words, the Mother of God stretched out her hands, and brilliant rays of light poured forth from them, which penetrated the earth and turned it into a sea of fire. The children were standing on the edge of the earth, which had opened up into an inferno. In her memoirs, Lucia describes the vision:

> Plunged in this fire were demons and souls in human form, all blackened or burnished bronze, floating about in the conflagration, now raised into the air by the flames that issued from within themselves together with great clouds of smoke, now falling back on every side like sparks in huge fires, without weight or equilibrium, amid shrieks and groans of pain and despair, which horrified us and made us tremble with fear. . . . The demons could be distinguished by their terrifying and repellent likeness to frightful and unknown animals, black and transparent like burning coals.

Looking with kindness at the frightened children, Our Lady explained, "You have seen where the souls of poor sinners go. To save them, God wishes to establish in the world the devotion to my Immaculate Heart. If people do what I tell you, many souls will be saved and there will be peace." Our Lady told them that the war would come to an end soon, but unless people stopped offending God, a worse war would break out under the pontificate of Pope Pius XI. She predicted, "When you see a night illumined by an unknown light, know that this is the great sign given you by God that he is about to punish the world for its crimes, by means of war, famine, and persecutions of the Church and of the Holy Father."

In order to prevent this, the Blessed Mother asked for the consecration of Russia to her Immaculate Heart and the Communion of Reparation on the First Saturdays. She added, "If my requests are heeded, Russia will be converted, and there will be peace. If not, she will spread her errors throughout the world, causing wars and persecutions of the Church. The good will be martyred and the Holy Father will have much to suffer, various nations will be annihilated. In the end, my Immaculate Heart will triumph."

The Blessed Mother also requested the children to say the following prayer after each decade of the Rosary: "O my Jesus, forgive us, save us from the fire of hell. Lead all souls to heaven, especially those who are in most need [of thy mercy]." Our Lady asked that the children keep everything she revealed to them a secret until she granted them permission to share it with others. With that, she disappeared.

Mary shared three secrets with the children. The first secret was the vision of hell. The second secret was Our Lady's warning about the coming Second World War and the rise of communism in Russia. The third secret was the vision that the children had of events that would take place during World War II and the Cold War.

The children had a prophetic vision that was not revealed publicly until the beatification Mass of Francisco and Jacinta on May 13, 2000. It was a symbolic vision of a future event. Lucia described the vision as follows:

> At the left of Our Lady and a little above, we saw an Angel with a flaming sword in his left hand; flashing, it gave out flames that looked as though they would set the world on fire; but they died out in contact with the splendor that Our Lady radiated towards him from her right hand: pointing to the earth with his right hand, the Angel cried out in a loud voice: "Penance, Penance, Penance!" And we saw in an immense light that is God: "something similar to how people appear in a mirror when they pass in front of it" a Bishop dressed in White "we had the impression that it was the Holy Father." Other Bishops, Priests, men and women Religious going up a steep mountain, at the top of which there was a big Cross of rough-hewn trunks as of a cork-tree with the bark; before reaching there the Holy Father passed through a big city half in ruins and half trembling with halting step, afflicted with pain and sorrow, he prayed for the souls of the corpses he met on his way; having reached the top of the mountain, on his knees at the foot of the big Cross he was killed by a group of soldiers who fired bullets and arrows at him, and in the same way there died one after another the other Bishops, Priests,

men and women Religious, and various lay people of different ranks and positions. Beneath the two arms of the Cross there were two Angels each with a crystal aspersorium in his hand, in which they gathered up the blood of the Martyrs and with it sprinkled the souls that were making their way to God.

Interpretation of Images and Words

The Angel With the Flaming Sword

In a theological commentary that is included in the Vatican's declaration concerning *The Message of Fatima*, Joseph Cardinal Ratzinger explained the meaning of the vision of the angel:

> The angel with the flaming sword on the left of the Mother of God recalls similar images in the Book of Revelation. This represents the threat of judgement which looms over the world. Today the prospect that the world might be reduced to ashes by a sea of fire no longer seems pure fantasy: man himself, with his inventions, has forged the flaming sword. The vision then shows the power which stands opposed to the force of destruction—the splendor of the Mother of God and, stemming from this in a certain way, the summons to penance.

The Mountain, the City in Ruins, and the Cross

In his commentary, then Cardinal Ratzinger explained these symbols:

> The place of the action is described in three symbols: a steep mountain, a great city reduced to ruins and finally a large rough-hewn cross. The mountain and city symbolize the arena of human history: history as an arduous ascent to the summit, history as the arena of human creativity and social harmony, but at the same time a place of destruction, where man actually destroys the fruits of his own work. The city can be the place of communion and progress, but also of danger and the most extreme menace. On the mountain stands the cross—the goal and guide of history. The cross transforms destruction into salvation; it stands as a sign of history's misery but also as a promise for history.

Penance, Penance, Penance!

Metanoia is a term used in the Greek New Testament in the preaching of the apostles that means a radical change of heart, a turning away from sin to the practice of virtue. It involves remorse, repentance, and atonement. St. Augustine, who lived a life of licentiousness in his youth, but who underwent a radical conversion in later life, experienced metanoia. Another example of metanoia is St. Paul, who was previously known as Saul (his Hebrew name). Saul was active in persecuting Christians and was there when St. Stephen, the first martyr, was stoned to death. One day, while riding his horse on the way to Damascus to arrest more Christians, the Lord blinded him with a light so bright that it knocked him to the ground. Then he heard a voice from heaven that said, "Saul, Saul, why do you persecute me?" Stunned, Saul asked, "Who are you Lord?" It was then that Jesus revealed himself to the man who would go from being one of Christ's greatest opponents to one of his great champions. "I am Jesus, whom you are persecuting" (Acts 9:4–6). Saul was blind and unable to eat or drink for three days. The Lord commanded Ananias to go and minister to Saul. After Ananias laid hands on him, the "scales fell from his eyes" and he was baptized (Acts 9:18).

From that time forward, Saul preached the good news of Christ. Along with his new life, Saul later began using his Roman name, Paul. Saul had experienced a radical change of heart, which greatly altered his behavior. He changed his life and became an apostle for Jesus Christ.

Penance is the call to offer sacrifice to the Lord in atonement for our sins and for those of others. The message that we hear in the bible— "repent and believe in the gospel" (Mk 1:15)—is the core of the message of Fatima. The Mother of God, in all her apparitions, encourages us to pray and practice penance, to turn away from our sinful ways—as did Paul—and turn back to God, who, in his loving mercy, will forgive us and draw us close to him.

The Bishop Dressed in White

Many of the popes during the twentieth century suffered greatly, but perhaps no one suffered as much as Pope St. John Paul II, who fought communism, dealt with the clergy abuse scandal, and sought to supplant the culture of death with a culture of life.

His was a life of great suffering and loss, loss which began with the deaths of his mother and older brother as a child, and later that of his father when the future pope was a young adult. He was, however, destined to be a courageous, charismatic leader, whom others sought to remove from his position due to his strong influence, which threatened atheistic communistic ideals.

Much insight into Sister Lucia's thoughts concerning the visions was gleaned through a meeting between Sister Lucia, Archbishop Tarcisio Bertone, then Secretary of the Congregation for the Doctrine of the Faith, and Bishop Serafim de Sousa Ferreira e Silva, bishop of Leiria-Fatima on Thursday, April 27, 2000, in the Carmel of Saint Teresa in Coimbra, a record of which is included along with Cardinal Ratzinger's aforementioned commentary. When asked if the principal figure in the vision was the pope, Sister Lucia said that it was. "We did not know the name of the Pope; Our Lady did not tell us the name of the Pope; we did not know whether it was Benedict XV or Pius XII or Paul VI or John Paul II; but it was the Pope who was suffering and that made us suffer too." With regard to the Holy Father—that is, the Bishop dressed in white who, in the vision, is struck dead and falls to the ground—Sister Lucia indicated that she was in full agreement with John Paul II's belief that "it was a mother's hand that guided the bullet's path and in his throes the Pope halted at the threshold of death."

But what exactly happened on that day that Pope St. John Paul II's life was nearly taken by an assassin's bullet? On the sixty-fourth anniversary of the feast of Our Lady of Fatima on May 13, 1981, in St. Peter's Square, assassin Mehmet Ali Agca shot and wounded Pope John Paul II after escaping from a Turkish prison. The bullet missed his central aorta by only a few millimeters. Had it hit his heart, the Holy Father would have died instantly. While in the hospital, Pope St. John Paul II read and reviewed the Church's documentation of Fatima and the Third Secret of Fatima. He was convinced that Our Lady of Fatima had saved his life. He believed that it was her hand that prevented the bullet from entering his heart and killing him. On the first anniversary of the assassination attempt, he visited her at Fatima to thank her for saving his life. He also made two more visits to Fatima to express his gratitude. Ultimately, on March 25, 1984, in order to fulfill the request of Our Lady of Fatima, the pope consecrated the world—including Russia—to the Immaculate Heart of Mary. Sister Lucia personally confirmed that this solemn and universal act of consecration corresponded to what Our Lady desired. Shortly thereafter, communism in Russia collapsed.

Though replete with apocalyptic images and the aforementioned vision of hell, ultimately, Our Lady's message is one of hope if we live as we should. She has told us that, in the end, her Immaculate Heart will triumph. Cardinal Ratzinger in his commentary explained this promise to us:

> The Heart open to God, purified by contemplation of God, is stronger than guns and weapons of every kind. The fiat of Mary, the word of her heart, has changed the history of the world, because it brought the Savior into the world—because, thanks to her Yes, God could become man in our world and remains so for all time. The Evil One has power in this world, as we see and experience continually; he has power because our freedom continually lets itself be led away from God. But since God himself took a human heart and has thus steered human freedom towards what is good, the freedom to choose evil no longer has the last word. From that time forth, the word that prevails is this: "In the world you will have tribulation, but take heart; I have overcome the world" (Jn 16:33).

The Frustrated Apparition

August 13, 1917

The enemies of the Church—the atheistic civil authorities—began to feel threatened by the children and their visions. With the revolution of 1910, the Freemasons had overthrown the king of Portugal, seized power, banished all religious from the country, and were incessantly persecuting the Church by creating immoral laws. Now this new religious movement at Fatima had threatened to destroy all the hard work of dechristianization that had taken them years to accomplish.

After the July apparition, people had become even more interested in the apparitions at Fatima. The children told everyone that Our Lady had revealed a secret to them and that there would be a great miracle in October to prove that the visions were indeed authentic. This news stirred up great curiosity and interest throughout Portugal and even beyond its borders. Thus, the civil authorities were determined to disprove the children and prevent them from going to the apparition site.

Consequently, the mayor of Ourém, Arturo de Olivreira Santos—a fallen-away Catholic and a Freemason—kidnapped the children and imprisoned them. He threatened to burn them alive in boiling oil if they did not reveal the secret Our Lady shared with them. Despite his efforts, the children refused to disclose any information to him.

On the next scheduled apparition of August 13, an estimated eighteen thousand people showed up to witness the event. They prayed the Rosary and sang hymns. At the appointed time of the apparitions, they heard a loud explosion followed by a flash of lightning. The sun grew dim, and a beautiful array of colors filled the sky. A luminous white

cloud appeared above the holm oak tree, remained there for a moment, rose, and then disappeared. While the crowd was disappointed that the children were not at the Cova, they knew that they had experienced something miraculous there.

On August 15, the Solemnity of the Assumption of the Blessed Virgin Mary into Heaven, the children were finally set free. Santos had one of his men drive the children back to Fatima where they were left on the steps of the parish rectory. A group of people was arriving for Mass at the time the children were dropped off, and when they saw this, they were very angry with the driver. Some even suspected that the pastor was involved with the kidnapping, as they had seen the children at the rectory prior to their abduction. However, Ti Marto, the father of Francisco and Jacinta, was there to calm them down and to reassure them that God allowed this situation to happen to the visionaries for a reason.

The Next Three Apparitions

THE FOURTH APPARITION–AUGUST 19, 1917

On Sunday, August 19, Lucia, Francisco, and his brother John were grazing their flock near the village of Valinhos. Around four o'clock in the afternoon, the sun dimmed, the air grew cool, and the three children saw a flash of light. Jacinta was not with them, so Lucia had John run home to get her. This time Our Lady's visit was short. She asked the children to come to the Cova da Iria on the thirteenth and to continue to pray the Rosary daily. She again promised that she would perform a miracle in October so that everyone would believe.

The Blessed Mother told them that she was displeased by the actions of the mayor and that, consequently, the miracle that she promised for October would not be as magnificent as originally planned.

She concluded the visit by reminding the children to pray and sacrifice: "Pray, pray very much and make sacrifice for sinners; for many souls go to hell, because there are none to sacrifice themselves and to pray for them."

THE FIFTH APPARITION–SEPTEMBER 13, 1917

On September 13, approximately thirty thousand people showed up for the fifth apparition. People flung themselves in front of the children, begging them to present their prayer petitions to Our Lady.

At noon, the sun dimmed to such an extent that even the stars became visible. As the children prayed the Rosary, they saw a flash of light, and Our Lady appeared over the holm oak tree. Those present saw a globe of light over the tree and the branches of the tree bend as if someone were standing on them. Onlookers also saw white petals fall from the sky, which dissolved before reaching the ground. They heard Lucia speak to an invisible being. Those closest to the tree reported that they heard the whispering of the apparition.

Our Lady told the children, "Continue to pray the Rosary in order to obtain the end of the war. In October, Our Lord will come, as well as Our Lady of Dolours (Sorrows) and Our Lady of Mount Carmel. Saint Joseph will appear with the Child Jesus to bless the world. God is pleased with your sacrifices." Lucia asked her to cure several sick people. Our Lady replied that she would heal some, but not all.

THE SIXTH APPARITION: THE MIRACLE OF THE SUN– OCTOBER 13, 1917

October 13, 1917 fell on a Sunday, and at midday, a crowd of approximately one hundred thousand spectators gathered on a rainy day in a wet, muddy field to witness the miracle that was about to take place. The people had gathered there because the children had revealed that Our Lady would perform a great miracle at Cova da Iria to prove that the visions were authentic.

Shortly after noon, a flash of light appeared over the holm oak tree. The crowd grew quiet and quickly fell to their knees. Suddenly, she appeared. Our Lady was dressed in white with brilliant beams of radiant light emanating from her body. She rested her luminous white feet upon the small evergreen tree, which was adorned with flowers and ribbons.

Lucia asked, "What do you want of me?"

Our Lady answered, "I wish to tell you that I want a chapel built here in my honor. I am the Lady of the Rosary. Continue to pray the Rosary every day. The war is going to end, and the soldiers will soon return to their homes."

Lucia said, "I have many things to ask you: the cure of some sick persons, the conversion of sinners, and some other things. . ."

The Sanctuary of Fatima

In the apparitions of 1917, the Mother of God made a request that would forever change the landscape of a tiny hamlet in Portugal, making it one of the preeminent pilgrimage destinations in the world. In response to Our Lady's request that a "chapel . . . be built here in my honor," the first little one was constructed in 1919 where the apparitions occurred at the Cova da Iria. As the years have passed and pilgrims continue to arrive by the millions each year, the shrine has grown steadily.

Today, the Sanctuary of Fatima includes the Basilica of Our Lady of the Rosary, including its Chapel of the Lausperene, a great oak tree (near where the apparitions occurred), a monument to the Sacred Heart of Jesus, and the Chapel of the Apparitions on the exact spot where the visionaries were first visited by Mary. Many other buildings and monuments have arisen over the years to commemorate the events which took place there one hundred years ago. Perhaps the most interesting is the part of the Berlin Wall that was moved to Fatima to mark the role of Our Lady in the momentous events which led to its fall and that of communism.

As Fatima received more and more pilgrims, the Basilica of Our Lady of the Rosary was no longer large enough to accommodate them all, and so the much larger Basilica of the Holy Trinity was built across from the main sanctuary.

One suspects that the Blessed Mother and the three children of Fatima to whom she came would be pleased with how well they and those who came after them responded to her request that a "chapel be built there in her honor."

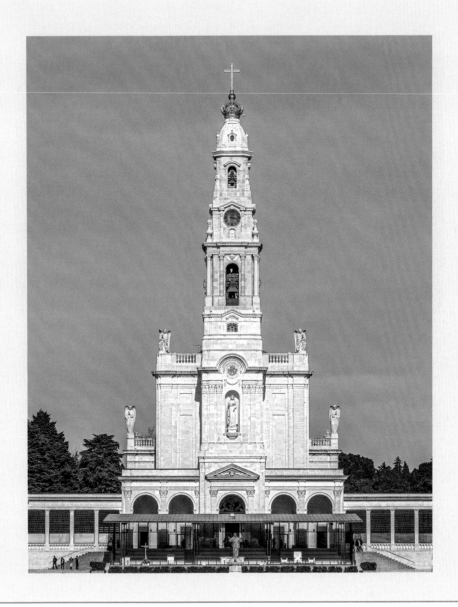

Our Lady responded, "Some yes, but not others. They must amend their lives and ask forgiveness for their sins." Looking very sad, she added, "Do not offend the Lord our God anymore because He is already so much offended." Then, as Our Lady opened her hands, they began glowing, and as she stood up, her own radiant rays bonded with the bright blaze of the sun and she disappeared.

At that moment, Lucia cried out, "Look at the sun!"

Once Our Lady had disappeared and Lucia had told the crowd to look at the sun, three visions followed in succession, which symbolized the Joyful, Sorrowful, and Glorious Mysteries. Lucia alone viewed all three visions; Francisco and Jacinta saw only the first.

First, St. Joseph appeared with the Child Jesus and Our Lady of the Rosary. It was the Holy Family. The Virgin was dressed in white with a blue mantle. St. Joseph was also dressed in white, and the Child Jesus in light red. The foster father of Our Lord blessed the crowd. The Child Jesus did the same.

Then there was a vision of Our Lady of Sorrows and Our Lord overwhelmed with sorrow on the way to Calvary. Our Lord made the sign of the cross to bless the people.

Finally, Our Lady of Mount Carmel, crowned queen of heaven and earth, appeared in a glorious vision holding a brown scapular in her hand and the Child Jesus on her knee. While these three visions transpired, the crowd witnessed the miracle of the sun. It had rained throughout the apparition.

Meanwhile, the crowd had stood up and looked at the sky, entranced by an amazing array of visions. The clouds parted, exposing the sun as an enormous silver disc, shining with extreme intensity. Then, the huge disk started to "dance." The sun spun swiftly like a revolving ball of fire. Then it stopped abruptly for a moment, only to start spinning again. Its outer edges turned scarlet red; spinning, it scattered its fiery flames across the sky. The reflection of the flames changed the colors of everything around them—the trees, the people, the earth, and even the air. Shimmering shades of yellow, blue, and white colors painted the environment. Finally, the ball of fire trembled, shook, and then plunged in a zigzag pattern toward the terrified crowd. Fearing that this was the end of the world, the people dropped to their knees and cried out in unison, weeping and praying, begging God to have mercy on them.

All this lasted about ten minutes. Finally, the sun zigzagged back to its original spot in the sky and returned to normal. Surprisingly, people noticed that their clothes, soaking wet from the rain, had dried. The miracle of the sun was also seen by several witnesses up to twenty-five miles away from the apparition site.

The Portugal news and other newspapers at that time reported the miraculous event.

On October 13, 1930, before a crowd of more than one hundred thousand pilgrims at the Cova da Iria, the bishop of Leiria read his pastoral letter that ended with the following declaration: "We deem it well: 1. to declare worthy of belief the vision of the shepherds at the Cova da Iria, in the Parish of Fatima, of this Diocese, on the thirteenth day of the months from May to October, 1917; 2. to give official permission for the cult of Our Lady of Fatima."

O MILAGRE DE FÁTIMA

Varios aspectos do povo ajoelhado e orando no momento de descobrir o sol e de se dar o fenomeno que tanto impressionou a multidão.

no vagalhão colossal d'aquele povo que ali se juntou a 13 de outubro. O teu racionalismo sofreu um formidavel embate e quer-s estabelecer uma opinião segura socorrendo-te de depoimentos insuspeitos como o meu, pois que estive lá apenas no desempenho de uma missão bem dificil, tal a de relatar imparcialmente para um grande diario, O Seculo, os factos que diante de mim se desenrolassem e tudo quanto de curioso e de elucidativo a eles se prendesse. Não ficará por satisfazer o teu desejo, mas decerto que os nossos olhos e os nossos ouvidos não viram nem ouviram coisas diversas, e que raros foram os que ficaram insensiveis á grandeza de semelhante espectaculo, unico entre nós e de todo o ponto digno de meditação e de estudo..

(Carta a alguem que pede um testemunho insuspeito).

Quebrando um silencio de mais de vinte anos e com a invocação dos longinquos e saudosos tempos em que convivemos n'uma fraternal camaradagem, iluminada então p'la fé comum e fortalecida por identicos propositos, escreves-me para que te diga, sincera e minuciosamente, o que vi e ouvi na charneca de Fátima, quando a fama de celestes aparições congregou n'aquele desolado ermo dezenas de milhares de pessoas mais sedentas, segundo creio, de sobrenatural do que impelidas por mera curiosidade ou receosas de um logro... Estão os catolicos em desacordo sobre a importancia e a significação do que presenceram. Uns convenceram-se de que se tinham cumprido prometimentos do Alto; outros acham-se ainda longe de acreditar na incontroversa realidade de um milagre. Foste um crente na tua juventude e deixaste de sel-o. Pessoas de familia arrastaram-te a Fátima,

O que ouvi e me levou a Fátima? Que a Virgem Maria, depois da festa da Ascensão, aparecera a tres crianças que apascentavam gado, duas mocinhas e um zagalete, recomendando-lhes que orassem e prometendo-lhes aparecer ali, sobre uma azinheira, no dia 13 de cada mez, até que em outubro lhes daria qualquer sinal do poder de Deus e faria revelações. Espalhou-se a nova por muitas leguas em ma

redondeza; voou, de terra em terra, até os confins de Portugal, e a roma-

Illness and Death Come for Two Visionaries

FRANCISCO

Following the first apparition on May 13, 1917, Francisco knew that he would be dying soon—as Our Lady had predicted—and became more faithful in prayer. He showed little interest in attending school but preferred instead to make frequent visits to the Blessed Sacrament. He was also very conscientious in praying the Rosary daily.

In October 1918, Francisco became seriously ill during an influenza epidemic. Throughout his illness, he offered up continual sacrifices to console Jesus who was offended by so many sins. As his illness grew worse, he no longer had the strength to pray the Rosary. Nevertheless, he remained focused on Jesus and eternal life. He knew his time was short. During his final days of this life, he cried out to his father, pleading with him to receive Our Lord in Holy Communion. When he prepared himself to receive the sacrament of Reconciliation for the first time, he asked Lucia and Jacinta to help him remember his sins. Following his

confession, he made his first Holy Communion. Unable to recite the Rosary due to weakness, he asked Jacinta and Lucia to pray the Rosary loudly so that he could focus on it rather than his own suffering and follow along mentally.

Two days later, close to death, he called out, "Look mamma, look, a light so beautiful, there near the door." On April 4, 1919, around ten o'clock in the evening, he passed on peacefully to paradise. Sister Lucia recalls in her memoirs, "He flew away to Heaven in the arms of our Heavenly Mother." He was beatified by Pope St. John Paul II on May 13, 2000.

Jacinta's Illness and Death

On July 13, 1917, the children were shown a horrifying scene of hell in which they saw countless souls immersed in an immense fire. When Jacinta saw this vision and heard Our Lady say, "Pray for sinners, many go to Hell because there is no one to pray for them," she quickly developed within her heart a burning love for God and the souls of her fellow men.

For four years, Jacinta offered herself as a living sacrifice to please God and Our Lady and to save souls. Lucia writes in her memoirs how Jacinta never tired of telling Our Lord and Our Lady how much she loved them. She even said, "I have a fire in my chest but it doesn't burn me."

The Immaculate Heart of Mary

Historically, traditional devotion to the Immaculate Heart of Mary began in the twelfth century in the writings of St. Anselm and St. Bernard of Clairvaux. St. Bernardine of Siena also promoted this devotion in the fifteenth century. St. John Eudes began celebrating the feast of the Pure Heart of Mary on February 8, 1643—two decades before the liturgical feast of the Sacred Heart of Jesus was celebrated. In the nineteenth century, Popes Pius VII and Pius IX permitted several churches to celebrate the feast of the Pure Heart of Mary. The apparitions at Fatima in 1917 emphasized the devotion of the Immaculate Heart of Mary as the Mother of Mercy, Refuge of Sinners. Mary asked that Russia be consecrated to her Immaculate Heart. In response to this request, Pope Pius XII consecrated the world to our Blessed Mother in 1942 and then, in 1944, established the feast of the Immaculate Heart of Mary for the whole Church in order to obtain through her intercession "peace among nations, freedom for the Church, the conversion of sinners, the love of purity and the practice of virtue."

The Immaculate Heart of Mary at Fatima and Its Meaning

On June 13, 1917, Our Lady told the oldest of the visionaries, Lucia dos Santos, "My Immaculate Heart will be your refuge and the way that will lead you to God."

Thus, Mary is our refuge from sin. She is the one who protects us from the evils that fill our world and the one who acts as a mediatrix and an advocate of God's graces. She is a merciful mother who leads us to her Son for healing, conversion, and repentance. We need never fear anything when we place ourselves under the mantle of our Holy Mother and consecrate ourselves to her Immaculate Heart.

She offered up all her sufferings from the time of the June apparition at age seven until her death due to tuberculosis shortly before her eleventh birthday. In other words, to free souls from the fires of hell, Jacinta offered up many penances and sufferings. In the sizzling summer heat, she fasted from all drinking water. She also gave up her lunch and afternoon snacks, which she presented to children who were poorer than she. To save souls, she wore a rough piece of knotted rope next to her bare skin. One year after the apparitions, she became ill with influenza. She also suffered greatly from bronchial pneumonia and an abscess on her lung. However, she joyfully mentioned that her sickness was simply a new opportunity to suffer for the conversion of sinners and the salvation of souls.

Jacinta was hospitalized for two months. While she was there, only once were members of her family able to visit her; her mother and Lucia came and remained with her for two days. During that time, she suffered joyfully, talking about how happy she was to suffer for the love of God, the Immaculate Heart of Mary, the conversion of sinners, and the Holy Father. Since she was showing no improvement in the hospital, the physicians unanimously decided that it would be better for her to return home with her family and dismissed her at the end of August.

Our Lady visited Jacinta during her stay at home. She tearfully shared the story of the visit with Lucia. Our Lady told Jacinta that she wanted her to go to another hospital in Lisbon. She told Jacinta she would never see her parents or Lucia again, but would die alone. However, Our Lady also reassured Jacinta, telling her not to be afraid because she would take her to heaven.

Jacinta showed no improvement in her health at home, but only grew worse. An ulcerous sore was discovered on her chest. She was no longer able to eat or drink, and her small frame had become skeleton-like. At the recommendation of the family doctor and their parish priest, her parents agreed to admit her into the Lisbon hospital where she would receive more specialized treatment and care. Jacinta arrived there on February 2, 1920; she was placed under the care of one of the hospital's most prominent specialists of children's diseases. A short time later, she was diagnosed with tuberculosis. For the next several days, she suffered intensely from this terrible disease.

On February 20, 1920, Our Lady kept her promise and took Jacinta to heaven. She was beatified along with Francisco on May 13, 2000.

On March 23, 2017, Pope Francis accepted the second miracle attributed to the intercession of Blesseds Francisco and Jacinta Marto. The approval of a second miracle is required in the canonization process. Thus, the two shepherd children of Fatima may now be declared saints of God's Church, in fact, may already have been declared so by the time this book is printed. It is only too appropriate that—among the many dramatic and miraculous events associated with the Fatima apparitions and their aftermath—this, the acceptance of a second miracle opening the way to their canonization, occur during the hundredth anniversary of Our Lady's appearances to the children.

Convents, Continuing Apparitions, and Contemplation

After the deaths of Jacinta and Francisco, Lucia alone remained to carry on the mission assigned by Our Lady. She yearned for their company, but reminded herself of the words of the woman from heaven, who reassured her that she would never be alone. However, it was difficult for her to face the unending stream of visitors who came to the apparition site and to her home at all hours of the day and night, demanding to speak with her. Her life was anything but peaceful.

The Reverend Joseph Correia da Silva, who was appointed bishop of the Diocese of Leiria in Portugal in 1920, had heard of the continual stream of steady visitors who disturbed Lucia and her family. He wanted to send her to a convent school where she would be unknown and free from all these intrusions. At fourteen, she entered boarding school at the convent of the Sisters of St. Dorothy in Vilar, near Oporto in the northern part of Portugal. In the June 1917 apparition, Our Lady stated that she wanted Lucia to learn to read. Lucia began attending school for the first time after the apparitions. She got off to a late start, but with her aptitude, excellent memory, and determination, she acquired a fairly comprehensive education.

On October 24, 1925, at the age of eighteen, Lucia entered the Institute of the Sisters of St. Dorothy as a postulant in the convent in Pontevedra, Spain, where Our Lady—as she promised in 1917—revealed to her the first part of God's plan for the salvation of sinners. She made her first vows on October 3, 1928, and her perpetual vows on October 3, 1934, receiving the name Sister Mary of the Sorrowful Mother. Throughout this time, during which she moved to a convent in nearby Tuy, she continued to receive private revelations regarding the message of Fatima.

On December 10, 1925, Our Lady, with the Child Jesus by her side, appeared to Lucia in her room at the convent. Our Lady placed one hand upon Lucia's shoulder and, with the other hand, held a heart covered with sharp thorns. The Child Jesus said, "Have compassion on the Heart of Your Most Holy Mother. It is covered with the thorns [with] which ungrateful men pierce it at every moment, and there is no one to remove them with an act of reparation." Then, Our Lady spoke, "My daughter, look at my Heart encircled with the thorns [with] which ungrateful men pierce it at every moment by their blasphemies and ingratitude. Do you at least try to console me and announce in my name that I promise to assist at the hour of death with the graces necessary for salvation all those who, on the first Saturday of five consecutive months go to confession and receive Holy Communion, recite the Rosary and keep me company for a quarter of an hour while meditating on the mysteries of the Rosary with the intention of making reparation to me."

The Five First Saturdays

A core message of the revelations of Our Lady of Fatima concerns penance and making reparation. Chief among those sins for which we are asked to make reparation are the five ways in which people offend and blaspheme against the Immaculate Heart of Mary. As Our Lady tells us, those offenses are:

1. Offenses or blasphemies against the Immaculate Conception—its denial and/or ridicule.

2. Against her perpetual virginity—that she had relations with Joseph and had other children.

3. Against her divine maternity, refusing at the same time to accept her as mother of all mankind—denying that she is the Mother of God and our mother.

4. The implantation into children's hearts of indifference, contempt, and even hate against our Immaculate Mother.

5. Insults directed against her sacred images—displays of indifference or ridicule and the infliction of damage to them.

Practicing the Five First Saturday Communions of Reparation

With the specific intention of making reparation for offenses committed against the Immaculate Heart of Mary we need to: go to confession, receive Holy Communion worthily, and pray five decades of the Rosary.

We should keep Our Lady company for fifteen minutes while meditating on the mysteries of the Rosary. In addition to praying the Rosary, we need to meditate an additional fifteen minutes on the Mysteries (or Mystery) of the Rosary. Our Lady specifically requested this extra time of meditation when she spoke to Lucia: "Recite five decades of the Rosary, and keep me company for fifteen minutes while meditating on the mysteries of the Rosary." In this way, we meditate on the life of Jesus.

Lucia was deeply moved by the vision of Our Lady's bleeding heart. She shared this private revelation with her confessor and her superior, who, however, felt incapable of promoting the devotion.

Two months later, on February 15, 1926, the Child Jesus once again appeared to Lucia and questioned if she had spread the devotion of the reparation of the Immaculate Heart of Mary. Lucia told Jesus that she had shared it with her confessor and her superior, but her mother superior was unable to spread it on her own. Our Lord replied, "It is true that your superior alone can do nothing, but with my grace she can do all."

In the meantime, Lucia did her best to encourage others—specifically her mother—to become an advocate of this devotion of reparation to the Immaculate Heart of Mary. She also spoke to a priest, who remarked that Our Lord had used almost identical words to St. Margaret Mary when he spoke to her about his promises accompanying the Nine First Fridays.

In 1927, Our Lord appeared to Sister Lucia at her convent in Tuy as she was praying in the chapel. She asked Our Lord how she could answer questions from her superiors regarding the First Saturday devotions without divulging the Third Secret. It was then that she was given permission to divulge the first two parts of the Secret: the vision of hell and the devotion to the Immaculate Heart of Mary. She therefore informed her mother provincial, the bishop of Leiria, and another priest.

On June 13, 1929, the twelfth anniversary of the second apparition of Fatima, Our Lady asked for the consecration of Russia to her Immaculate Heart. Lucia was praying alone in the chapel at Tuy between 11 p.m. and midnight when she had a vision of the Trinity.

Suddenly the whole chapel was illumined with a supernatural light and above the altar appeared a cross of light, reaching to the ceiling. In a brighter light on the upper part of the cross, could be seen the face of a man as far as the waist; upon his breast was a dove of light; nailed to the cross was the body of another man. A little below the waist, I could see a chalice and a large host suspended in the air, on to which drops of blood were falling from the Face of Jesus Crucified and from the wound in His side. These drops ran down to the host and fell into the chalice. Beneath the right arm of the cross was Our Lady and in her hand was her Immaculate Heart. (It was Our Lady of Fatima, with her Immaculate Heart in her left hand, without sword or roses, but with a crown of thorns and flames). Under the left arm of the cross, large letters, as if of crystal clear water which ran down the altar, formed these words: "Grace and Mercy." I understood that it was the Mystery of the Most Holy Trinity which was shown to me, and I received lights about this mystery that I am not permitted to reveal.

Following the vision of the Trinity, Our Lady then asked for the consecration of Russia to her Immaculate Heart: "The moment has come in which God asks the Holy Father, in union with all the Bishops of the world, to make the consecration of Russia to my Immaculate Heart, promising to save it by this means. There are so many souls to whom the Justice of God condemns for sins committed against me, that I have come to ask reparation: sacrifice yourself for this intention and pray."

The Queen of Heaven and Earth promised the conversion of Russia to prevent war in the future and the spread of communism if two conditions were met: (1) if there was reparation via the First Saturday devotions and (2) if the Holy Father in union with all the bishops throughout the world would consecrate Russia to the Immaculate Heart of Mary.

Two years later, Our Lady again appeared to Lucia in the chapel to repeat her previous request of the consecration of Russia to her Immaculate Heart, adding, "If they heed my request, Russia will be converted and there will be peace." Our Lady reiterated that this consecration should be made by the pope in union with all the bishops of the world. Lucia once again shared Our Lady's appeal with her confessors. One of them, Fr. Jose Bernardo Goncalves, SJ, told her to write it down in a letter. He then showed Our Lady's request to the bishop. Two years passed and no progress was made.

At the end of May, 1930, Sister Lucia was praying before the Blessed Sacrament in the chapel at Tuy when she had a mystical experience with Our Lord. Her confessor had been asking her various questions such as why the Blessed Mother would request reparation on five consecutive Saturdays. Why not nine or seven? In response, Our Lord revealed five kinds of blasphemies and offenses spoken against the Immaculate Heart of Mary. Lucia describes them in her memoir. Our Lord concluded the conversation by telling Sister Lucia that those who commit these blasphemies are in grave danger of losing their souls and that reparation was necessary in order to move him to forgive them for these serious offenses.

In August of 1931, Sister Lucia was staying with a friend at Rianjo, Spain, a city near Pontevedra, to rest and recover from an illness. There in the small church of Our Lady of Guadalupe at Rianjo, Our Lord spoke to her as she was praying for the conversion of Spain, Portugal, and Russia. Our Lord criticized the tardiness of his ministers who delayed the consecration of Russia to the Immaculate Heart of Mary as requested by Our Lady of Fatima at Tuy two years and two months earlier. He said,

> You console me a great deal by asking for the conversion of those poor nations. Ask it also of My Mother frequently, saying: *Sweet Heart of Mary, be the salvation of Russia, Spain, Portugal, Europe, and the whole world.* At other times, say: *By thy pure and Immaculate Conception, O Mary, obtain for me the conversion of Russia, Spain, Portugal, Europe, and the whole world.*
>
> Make it known to my Ministers, given that they follow the example of the King of France in delaying the execution of my command (to consecrate Russia), they will follow him into misfortune. It will never be too late to have recourse to Jesus and Mary.

Our Lord was referring to the fact that, for one hundred years, the kings of France did not obey the command given by Jesus in 1689 to consecrate France to the Sacred Heart. King Louis XVI and his ministers were killed by revolutionaries, and that once most Catholic of countries—the "eldest daughter of the Church"—was plunged into the terror and violence of the French Revolution in 1789.

Nearly seven years passed. Then in late January, 1938, as Lucia looked out the windows of her convent in Galicia, Spain, one night, she saw the most extraordinary lights in the sky. She immediately recognized these lights as "the great sign"—the appearance of the "Great Northern Lights" that Our Lady of Fatima predicted that would signal that war was near. These were the lights that illuminated the skies throughout Europe on the night of January 25–26, 1938 during the hours of 8:45 p.m. to 1:15 a.m. The bright lights, which astronomers identified as an aurora borealis, appeared throughout the northern hemisphere, including locations as far south as North Africa, Bermuda, and California. However, this was no *common* aurora borealis.

The January 26, 1938 edition of the New York Times reported,

> From 6:30 to 8:30 P.M. the people of London watched two magnificent arcs rising in the east and west, from which radiated pulsating beams like searchlights in dark red, greenish blue and purple. . . . From an airplane the display looked like "a shimmering curtain of fire." . . . The phenomenon was seen as far south as Vienna. . . .
>
> [The phenomenon] spread fear in parts of Portugal and Lower Austria tonight, while thousands of Britons were brought running into the streets in wonderment. The ruddy glow led many to think half the city was ablaze. The Windsor Fire Department was called out in the belief that Windsor Castle was afire . . . an ill-omen for Scotland.
>
> The lights were clearly seen in Italy, Spain and even Gibraltar. . . .

Firemen turned out to chase non-existent fires. Portuguese villagers rushed in fright from their homes, fearing the end of the world. . . .

France, Jan. 25.—A huge blood-red beam of light . . . spread anxiety in numerous Swiss Alpine villages. Emblazoned in the northern sky the light brought thousands of telephone calls to Swiss and French authorities asking whether it was a fire, war or the end of the world. . . .

HAMILTON, Bermuda, Jan. 25.—The sky was brilliantly lighted with dark red streamers, flashing like searchlights.

After observing the "great sign," Sister Lucia wrote a letter to her bishop stating, "God made use of this to make me understand His justice was about to strike the guilty nations." In March 1938, Germany invaded Austria and the stage was set for World War II, which broke out in September 1939, six months after the death of Pope Pius XI.

Lucia Finds Solace in a Contemplative Community

In 1946, Lucia entered the Carmelite convent of St. Teresa in Coimbra where she made her profession as a Discalced Carmelite on May 31, 1949. She took the name Sister Maria Lucia of Jesus and the Immaculate Heart. It was here, within a contemplative community, that she found the solace and peace she had sought.

Over time, Sister Lucia would write two books: *Memoirs*, relating the events of Fatima in her own words, and *Calls from the Message of Fatima*, providing answers to the countless questions she was asked about living the message of Fatima.

The Popes and Fatima

POPE PIUS XI (1922–1939)

During the third apparition at Fatima, on July 13, 1917, Our Lady told the visionaries that World War I was going to end, "but if people do not cease offending God, a worse one will break out during the pontificate of Pius XI."

However, Pius XI did not become pope until 1922, which is a very significant fact in itself. How could the children even know that there was going to be a Pope Pius XI if some supernatural being had not told them?

Pope Pius XI, who was ordained to the priesthood in 1879, was an intelligent and highly educated man. He held three doctorates (in philosophy, canon law, and theology) from the Gregorian University in Rome. He worked as a professor, was an expert in the study of ancient Church manuscripts, and served as prefect of the Vatican library. Prior to being elected pope, he served as the apostolic nuncio to Poland.

He was also a very holy man who encouraged sacred devotions, sanctity, and world peace. As the bishop of Rome, Pius XI strongly encouraged devotion to the Sacred Heart. He canonized Bernadette Soubirous, Thérèse of Lisieux, John Vianney, John Fisher, Thomas More, and John Bosco. His papal motto—*The Peace of Christ in the Kingdom of Christ*—exemplified his efforts to seek world peace on the solid foundation of a renewed Christianity. He was certainly aware of the Fatima apparitions. However, for whatever reason, he did not promote devotion to Our Lady of Fatima nor did he consecrate the world to the Immaculate Heart of Mary. World War II began at the end of his papacy.

Pope Pius XII (1939–1958)

Born Eugenio Maria Giuseppe Giovanni Pacelli, the future Pope Pius XII was ordained in 1899 and entered papal diplomatic service in 1901. Prior to becoming pope, he served as nuncio to Bavaria and the German Republic and as papal secretary of state. He was elected pope in 1939 on the eve of World War II and had the difficult task of guiding the Church through that bloody conflict and through the postwar restoration as well.

Pope Pius XII was a strong Marian pope who had been a fervent follower of the Blessed Virgin Mary since childhood. He was consecrated as a bishop and elevated to archbishop at the same time on May 13, 1917, the day of the first apparition of Our Lady of Fatima.

His devotion to the Blessed Mother is perhaps best encapsulated in this quote recorded by the great Mariologist and catechist John Hardon, SJ, in a 1952 article for the *Review for Religious*. On the feast of the Immaculate Conception in 1939, Pius XII visited the church of St. Mary Major. He said at that time,

> If in Our rather long priestly life We have achieved anything good, anything felicitous, anything useful for the Catholic Faith, We do not glory in ourselves, but rather give honor to God and to Our Lady. Because We felt We were under Mary's protection, We have in hours of doubt and anxiety, of which We have had our full

share, called on Our beloved Mother. And Our call for her aid has never been in vain; We have always obtained from her the light, protection, and consolation that We asked for.

Pius amply repaid that debt by making significant contributions to Marian theology and devotion. In 1950, he proclaimed the dogma of the Assumption of the Blessed Virgin Mary, the belief of the Church that states that Mary, at the end of her earthly life, was assumed body and soul into heaven. In 1953, he wrote the encyclical *Fulgens Corona* ("Light the Crown"), announcing a Marian year for 1954, the centennial of the dogma of the Immaculate Conception. In the same year, he proclaimed the Queenship of Mary with his encyclical letter *Ad Caeli Reginam*, which was promulgated on October 11.

He also wrote many prominent passages on the Blessed Mother in his other encyclicals, such as *Mystici Corporis* ("The Mystical Body of Christ, the Church") and *Mediator Dei* ("On the Sacred Liturgy"). During his papacy, he canonized three saints associated with Marian devotion: St. Louis de Montfort, St. Anthony Mary Claret, and St. Catherine Labouré.

From the very beginning of his pontificate, he promoted veneration to the Mother of God among the faithful. In 1940, only one year after becoming pope, he approved the Fatima apparitions. Then, on October 31, 1942, in the silver jubilee year of Our Lady's apparitions at Fatima, Pope Pius XII consecrated the world to Mary's Immaculate Heart.

In a beautiful display of sacrificial devotion, on the occasion of the twenty-fifth anniversary of the Fatima apparitions, the women of Portugal offered up their valuable jewelry to create a crown for the Blessed Mother. The bishops of Portugal had decided to postpone the crowning

of Our Lady of Fatima until after the war was over. On May 13, 1946, Pope Pius XII, who was pleased to be associated with this ceremony, sent his delegate to represent him and crown Our Lady of Fatima as Queen of Portugal and Queen of the World.

Pope Pius XII continued to promote devotion to the Blessed Mother and encouraged families to pray the Rosary. In a radio message, the pope stated, "The Virgin Mother's insistence on the recitation of the family Rosary was meant to teach us that the secret of peace in family life lies in imitating the virtues of the Holy Family."

Pope John XXIII (1958–1963)

Pope John XXIII is best known for convening the Second Vatican Council. He was canonized by Pope Francis in St. Peter's Square on April 27, 2014, alongside the man who had beatified him, Pope St. John Paul II.

Born Angelo Giuseppe Roncalli at Sotto il Monte, Italy, the future pope was the fourth child of fourteen, born to pious parents. He entered the minor seminary in 1892 at the age of eleven, became a Secular Franciscan and entered the Pontifical Roman Seminary. On being ordained in 1904, he was appointed secretary to the bishop of Bergamo and taught in the seminary. He later served as a military chaplain during the First World War, a spiritual director of a seminary, and the Italian president of the Society for the Propagation of the Faith. In 1925, Pius XI elevated him to bishop and sent him to Bulgaria as the apostolic visitator. During the Second World War, he used his diplomatic means to save as many Jews as he could by obtaining safe passage for them. He was elevated to the cardinalate and named patriarch of Venice in 1953.

Elected pope on the death of Pope Pius XII, he was an example of a pastoral pope, a good shepherd who cared deeply for his sheep. He manifested this concern in his social encyclicals, especially *Pacem in Terris* ("On Peace in the World").

His greatest act as pope, however, was the inspiration to convoke the Second Vatican Council, which he opened on October 11, 1962. Pope John's spirit of humble simplicity, profound goodness, and deep life of prayer affected all that he did and inspired people to affectionately call him "Good Pope John."

John XXIII had a deep love for Our Lady and the Rosary. On December 13, 1962, he instituted the feast of Our Lady of the Rosary in honor of Our Lady of Fatima. His love for the most Marian of prayers was reflected in the following words he penned in his autobiography *Journal of a Soul: The Autobiography of Pope John XXIII*: "This is the rosary of Mary, considered in its various elements, which are linked together in vocal prayer and woven into it as in delicate and rich embroidery, full of spiritual warmth and beauty" (p. 360).

Although Pope John XXIII never visited Fatima as the Holy Father, he did visit it when he was Cardinal Roncalli on May 13, 1956. He read the Third Secret of Fatima but did not reveal it. While he was the Holy Father, the bishops discussed the necessity of consecrating the world to the Immaculate Heart of Mary but did not discuss Russia.

Pope Paul VI (1963–1978)

Following the death of Pope John XXIII, Pope Paul VI was elected to the Holy See on June 21, 1963. He was a strong devotee of the Blessed Virgin Mary. In his encyclical *Ecclesiam Suam* ("His Own Church") the Holy Father stated that he considered "devotion to the Mother of God as of paramount importance in living the life of the Gospel" (no. 58).

On the feast of the Presentation of the Blessed Virgin Mary on November 21, 1964, *Lumen Gentium* (Vatican II's Dogmatic Constitution on the Church, which defined the Church's role in relation to the modern world) was approved; it included a chapter on Mary. That afternoon, at the close of the third session of the Second Vatican Council, Pope Paul VI declared Mary to be the Mother of the Church and personally renewed his consecration to her. In his 1966 encyclical *Christi Matri* ("Mother of Christ"), Paul VI encouraged praying the Rosary in view of the Vietnam War and the threat of atomic weapons in the world. He also requested special prayers to the Blessed Mother under the title of Mary, Queen of Peace, writing,

> Nothing seems more appropriate and valuable to Us than to have the prayers of the whole Christian family rise to the Mother of God, who is invoked as the Queen of Peace, begging her to pour forth abundant gifts of her maternal goodness in midst of so many great trials and hardships. We want constant and devout prayers to be offered to her whom We declared Mother of the Church,

its spiritual parent, during the celebration of the Second Vatican Council, thereby winning the applause of the Fathers and of the Catholic world, and confirming a point of traditional doctrine.

On the fiftieth anniversary of the first apparition in Fatima, Paul VI made a pilgrimage there, the first ever visit by a pope. When the Holy Father arrived, he met with Sister Lucia, who had been permitted to leave her cloistered Carmelite monastery on this special occasion at the pope's request. She knelt at the Holy Father's feet for some time, while the crowd yelled, "Long live the pope!" and "Ave!" The pope knelt in front of the statue of Our Lady of Fatima, placed a rosary around her neck, and prayed for world peace. He then introduced Sister Lucia to the exuberant crowd. It has been recounted that she asked to speak privately with him. He reportedly responded, "As you see this is not the time" and asked her to communicate with him via her bishop.

On this fiftieth anniversary, the pope issued an apostolic exhortation to the bishops of the world, *Signum Magnum* ("The Great Sign"), in which he requested national, diocesan, and individual consecration to the Immaculate Heart of Mary. Paul VI died on August 6, 1978, the feast of the Transfiguration. He was beatified on October 19, 2014.

Paul VI was succeeded by Pope John Paul I. His pontificate lasted only one month before he passed on to eternal life; hence, he is known as "the September Pope." However, as patriarch of Venice (then Albino Luciani), he had gone on pilgrimage to Fatima in 1977 and visited with Sister Lucia.

POPE ST. JOHN PAUL II (1978–2005)

Karol (Charles) Jósef Wojtyła was born on
May 8, 1920, the feast of the Presentation of
the Blessed Virgin Mary, in the small town of
Wadowice, about thirty miles from Krakow,
Poland. His mother, who had been ill for many
years, died one month before his ninth birthday. Following her death, he developed a deep
prayer life and entrusted himself to the care
of his heavenly mother. As a young man, he
was introduced to the writings of St. Louis de
Monfort and his spiritual classic *True Devotion to the Blessed Virgin* while
working at the Solvay utilities plant. He later reflected, "I was already
convinced that Mary leads us to Christ, but at that time I began to realize also that Christ leads us to His Mother" (Evert, p. 165). Around the
age of twenty, he consecrated his life to the Blessed Virgin Mary.

This profound love for Mary, the Mother of God, was mirrored in
the personal motto referencing her that he adopted as pope: *Totus Tuus*—
that is, "All Yours." It was based on St. Louis de Montfort's prayer: "I am
all Thine and all that I have is Thine, O my sweet Jesus, through Mary,
Thy holy Mother." His deep devotion to Our Lady was also reflected in
his papal coat of arms, which contained an *M* for Mary placed below the
arm of the cross, signifying how Mary, the faithful mother and follower,
stood at the foot of the cross. More than any other pope, John Paul II
strongly advocated Marian consecration for everyone.

During his papacy, Pope St. John Paul II endorsed the Marian Sodal-
ity and the Legion of Mary. As pope, he made frequent visits to Marian
shrines and made more Marian pilgrimages than any of his predecessors,

stating, "It is precisely in this pilgrimage through space and time, and even more through the history of souls that Mary is present, sharing unlike any other creature in the mystery of Christ" (Nachef, p. 85).

John Paul II's key Marian documents were *Redemptoris Mater* ("Mother of the Redeemer") and *Rosarium Virginis Mariae* ("The Rosary of the Virgin Mary").

Redemptoris Mater, his sixth encyclical, was written in 1987 in association with the Marian year that began on Pentecost Sunday in 1987. The encyclical addressed the Blessed Mother's importance to women, ecumenism, the relationship between Mary and Jesus, Mary's presence in the pilgrim Church, and Mary as a model of faith.

Rosarium Virginis Mariae was an apostolic letter the Pope wrote in 2002, declaring the start of a Year of the Rosary, which was celebrated from October 2002 to October 2003. In it, Pope John Paul II gave the Church five new Mysteries of the Rosary: the Mysteries of Light, or the Luminous Mysteries.

Pope St. John Paul II has been called the "Pope of Fatima." More than any other pope, he promoted the devotion. Sister Lucia met him in 1982 and 1991 at the Carmelite monastery in Fatima. They would meet again when he beatified Jacinta and Francisco on the feast of Our Lady of Fatima in 2000.

The Holy Father's reading also convinced him that the consecration of Russia to the Immaculate Heart of Mary was an absolute necessity if the world was to be saved from war and atheistic communism. On June 7, 1981, one year after the assassination attempt on his life, while he was still recovering from his injuries, Pope St. John Paul II composed an "Act of Entrustment," consecrating the world and Russia to the Immaculate Heart of Mary. Here is a portion of that entrustment prayer:

Mother of all individuals and peoples, you know all their
sufferings and hopes. In your motherly heart you feel all
the struggles between good and evil, between light and
darkness, that convulse the world: accept the plea which
we make in the Holy Spirit directly to your heart, and
embrace with the love of the Mother and Handmaid of
the Lord those who most await this embrace, and [refer-
ence to Russia] those whose act of entrustment you too
wait in a particular way. Take under your motherly protection the whole human family, which with affectionate love we entrust to you, O Mother. May there dawn

for everyone the time of peace and freedom, the time of truth, of justice and of hope.

The Holy Father purposely chose the June 7, 1981 date, as it was the Solemnity of Pentecost, the commemoration of the Council of Constantinople—which confirmed the divinity of the Holy Spirit—and the anniversary of the Council of Ephesus, which proclaimed Mary to be the Mother of God. This consecration, however, did not fulfill Our Lady of Fatima's requests, as it was not made in union with all of the bishops in the world. Nevertheless, John Paul II did repeat the consecration three more times during his pontificate.

On May 13, 1982, Pope St. John Paul II made his first pilgrimage to Fatima in order to express his gratitude and appreciation to Our Lady for saving his life. On the second day of his pilgrimage to Portugal, the Holy Father visited the Shrine of Our Lady of Fatima to commemorate the first anniversary of the attempt on his life (which had occurred the year before at St. Peter's Square in Rome) and the sixty-fifth anniversary of Our Lady's first apparition there. At the Chapel of Apparitions of Fatima, he said,

> I saw in everything that was happening—I do not get tired of repeating it—a special maternal protection of Our Lady. And in this striking occurrence—and there are no mere coincidences in the designs of Divine Providence—I also saw an appeal and, perhaps, a call to attention for the message here sent and left, sixty-five years ago, through three children, born to humble people of the countryside, the little shepherds of Fatima, as they are universally known.

Our Lady of Fatima
Protects the Pope

On May 13, 1981, the anniversary of the first apparition of Fatima, John Paul II was conducting his regular Wednesday audience, riding in a white open jeep through St. Peter's Square. He had just taken a two-year-old girl into his arms, lifted her up for all to see, kissed her, and returned her to her parents with a wide smile when blasts from a pistol rang out. He collapsed into the arms of his secretary, Monsignor Dziwisz. The pope had been shot by Mehmet Ali Agca, a Turkish extremist. The pope was hit by four bullets from Agca's gun. One hit his right arm, another his left index finger, while the other two bullets lodged in his lower intestine.

Agca and his accomplice were arrested, and the Holy Father was moved to an ambulance, where he lost consciousness and was rushed to Gemelli Hospital in Rome. The surgeons operated for 5½ hours and were completely successful. His survival was miraculous. No vital organ had been damaged. The bullet had missed the main artery by a fraction of an inch. His personal physician said that it was as though the bullet had hit a steel wall and changed directions.

The Holy Father recovered, but later developed an infection and had to return to the hospital.

During this second stay at the hospital, he began to reflect on the assassination attempt and asked to see the Third Secret of Fatima. When he finished reading it, he began to realize his role in Fatima. He had been the pope dressed in white, and it was Our Lady of Fatima who had saved him. St. John Paul II said, "Someone's hand had shot me, but Another Hand directed the bullet. For in everything that happened to me on that very day, I felt that extraordinary motherly protection and care, which turned out to be stronger than the deadly bullet"

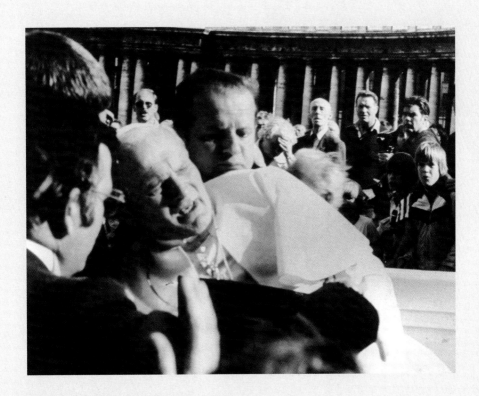

In his homily at Mass at Fatima that day, he stated that the message of Fatima was so "deeply rooted" in the Gospel message and in the tradition of the Church that it required a "commitment" on the part of the Church. He also spoke of Our Lady's spiritual motherhood, the need for the world to be consecrated to the Immaculate Heart of Mary. He encouraged everyone to pray the Rosary, in conjunction with Our Lady of Fatima's wishes. He reminded the faithful that the essential message of Fatima is "a call to conversion and repentance."

Following the Mass in Fatima, John Paul made an act of consecration of the modern world to Our Lady of Fatima. Unfortunately, this consecration was again not made in union with all the bishops of the world. But the Holy Father was clearly, inexorably, moving toward a consecration in conformity with the Our Lady's wishes made so long before. On October 16, 1983, John Paul renewed the Act of Consecration of the World to the Mother of God at the conclusion of the 1983 synod of bishops. Surrounded by numerous cardinals and bishops from all parts of the world who took part in it, he used the same prayer he said at the shrine of Fatima the previous year.

Then, finally, on March 25, 1984, the Pilgrim Virgin of Fatima statue traveled to the Vatican for a ceremony in St. Peter's Basilica. This time Pope St. John Paul II, in union with the bishops throughout the world, consecrated the world to the Immaculate Heart of Mary. Sister Lucia gave both her verbal and written approval of this consecration as fulfilling the conditions regarding the consecration of Russia set by Our Lady many years previously. After the Holy Father consecrated the world to the Immaculate Heart of Mary in 1984, some unexpected and dramatic political changes occurred in the world. In 1989, the Berlin Wall was taken down. Then, two years later, Soviet communism collapsed, the USSR was dissolved, and religious freedom was returned to Russia.

Pope St. John Paul continued his promotion of the Fatima message. On May 13, 1991, the Holy Father once again traveled to Portugal and prayed in front of the shrine statue of Our Lady of Fatima. In a strikingly symbolic act, he placed the bullet that had struck him ten years earlier into Our Lady's jeweled crown.

It was all too appropriate that on May 13, 2000, he who could be considered the "Fatima pope," returned to the little village in Portugal for the third and final time in order to beatify Francisco and Jacinta. The still-living visionary, Sister Lucia, was in attendance. Secretary of

State Angelo Cardinal Sodano read the transcript of the Third Secret aloud. The Vatican then published the transcript of the secret, attaching three other texts, including a theological commentary by Joseph Cardinal Ratzinger.

POPE BENEDICT XVI (2005–2013)

After the death of Pope St. John Paul II on April 2, 2005, and his funeral on April 8, Joseph Cardinal Ratzinger, as dean of the College of Cardinals, chaired the conclave to elect a new pope. The conclave opened on April 18, and Cardinal Ratzinger himself was elected pontiff on April 19, 2005. He chose the name Benedict after the founder of Western monasticism as well as Benedict XV who had led the Church through the tumultuous era of the First World War and had implored the victors in that struggle to be magnanimous in the terms offered to the vanquished. (Had he been heeded, perhaps the Second World War could have been avoided.)

Pope Benedict XVI was the third pope to visit the Fatima shrine, after Pope Paul VI in 1967 and Pope St. John Paul II's three trips in 1982, 1991, and 2000. In commemoration of the tenth anniversary of the beatification of Francisco and Jacinta, Benedict XVI visited Portugal from May 11–14, 2010.

The pontiff's first stop upon arriving by helicopter in Fatima was at the Chapel of Apparitions to pray and to give Our Lady a golden rose. The Holy Father stated that he brought with him a golden rose "as a homage of gratitude from the Pope for the marvels that the Almighty

has worked through you in the hearts of so many who come as pilgrims to this your maternal home." The pope also recalled the invisible hand that saved John Paul II. He said in a prayer to the Blessed Virgin Mary that "it is a profound consolation to know that you are crowned not only with the silver and gold of our joys and hopes, but also with the 'bullet' of our anxieties and sufferings."

On May 12, 2010, after Vespers at the Church of the Most Holy Trinity, Fatima, the Holy Father consecrated himself and all priests to the Immaculate Heart of Mary, entrusting them to her loving and powerful intercession. Later, after blessing candles on the esplanade of the Shrine of Our Lady of Fatima, he led thousands of pilgrims in the recitation of the holy Rosary in the Chapel of Apparitions.

The following day, May 13, the anniversary of the first apparition of Fatima, the Holy Father celebrated Mass at the same church. In his homily, speaking to a crowd of approximately five hundred thousand people, he said that it would be "mistaken" to consider the prophetic mission of the apparitions at Fatima complete. It continues to be relevant in that it continually invites men and women of good faith "to save the city of man." The pope stated that he had come to Fatima to pray for the human family.

The theme of his homily was one of hope. He invited all present "united in such great love and devotion at the feet of the Virgin, to rejoice fully in the Lord" so that "her merciful love" would serve as the "spring of our great hope." He added, "Hope is precisely what fills the demanding—yet at the same time comforting—Message that Our Lady left to us at Fatima."

In 2013, Benedict XVI became the first pope to resign since Gregory XII in 1415. In interviews, he stated that he felt that it was his duty to resign from the papacy due to his declining health and the rigorous demands of papal travel.

Pope Francis (2013–present)

Within the first year of his pontificate, Pope Francis focused the world's attention on Our Lady of Fatima. First, he consecrated his pontificate to her. Next, he consecrated World Youth Day 2013 to her. Then, on October 13, 2013, he consecrated the world to her.

October 13, 2013, marked the ninety-sixth anniversary of the Miracle of the Sun at Fatima. Before an estimated 150,000 pilgrims in St. Peter's Square, Pope Francis asked Mary to welcome the consecration "with the benevolence of a mother." "Guard our lives in your arms," he said. "Bless and strengthen every desire for goodness; revive and grow faith; sustain and illuminate hope; arouse and enliven charity; guide all of us on the path of holiness."

The Holy Father, like nearly all Latin American Catholics, has a strong devotion to the Blessed Mother. He even introduced the rest of the world to a favorite devotion of his: Our Lady under the title "Undoer of Knots." Yet there appears to be something very special about his affection for Mary as Our Lady of Fatima, an affection and devotion reflected in the words of his Act of Entrustment prayed on May 13, the Marian Day of the Year of Faith, 2013:

> Blessed Virgin Mary of Fatima, with renewed gratitude for your motherly presence we join in the voice of all generations that call you blessed.

> We celebrate in you the great works of God, who never tires of lowering himself in mercy over humanity, afflicted by evil and wounded by sin, to heal and to save it.

Accept with the benevolence of a Mother this act of entrustment that we make in faith today, before this your image, beloved to us.

As this book is being written, Pope Francis is planning a trip to Fatima on May 12–13, 2017, to mark the one hundredth anniversary of the apparitions of the Blessed Virgin Mary to three shepherd children in Cova da Iria. He will be the fourth pope to visit Fatima, following Pope Paul VI, Pope St. John Paul II, and Benedict XVI. His trip will be especially momentous as it is expected that he will then canonize the two little shepherd children of Fatima who died young. Blessed Francisco and Blessed Jacinta Marto will then be Saints Francisco and Jacinta.

Conclusion: The Centennial and Beyond

In 1917, Our Lady, the Mother of God, appeared to three simple, uneducated shepherd children from the obscure village of Aljustrel, Portugal, to give them a message that she wanted them to put into practice in their own lives and to proclaim to all mankind. Through her appearances at Fatima, Our Lady came to save the souls of her children from hell and to instruct those who would incline their hearts to her in the way to bring peace to a warring, broken, and godless world. Her message was one of warning but also one of hope.

It can be summed up in four sentences:

1. She told us that hell exists and that souls are being lost to it because there is no one to make reparation for their sins.

2. She said that war is a consequence of sin.

3. The salvation of souls and the attainment of world peace require the conversion of sinners. "People must

stop offending God because He is already so much offended." (October 13, 1917)

4. Her Immaculate Heart will triumph in the end. "My Immaculate Heart will be your refuge and the way that will lead you to God." (June 13, 1917)

It is deeply significant that the Fatima apparitions coincided with the Russian Revolution of 1917. The two events ran parallel to each other. Karl Marx influenced the Russian Revolution by publishing his book *The Communist Manifesto* on February 21, 1848, which detailed and

predicted a revolution in which the working-class proletariat eventually overthrew the ruling bourgeoisie. Atheism was at the root of Marxism. Marx was a militant atheist who believed that religion would distract people from taking part in the social revolution. Religion, Marx said, was the "opium of the people." In Marx's view, man is the supreme being, and religion prevents him from becoming aware of his true dignity and achieving his full potential; it drugs the mind and deludes it with concerns about an eternal afterlife. Thus, in Marx's view, religion retarded human growth and development. It was exactly this self-centered and fallacious ideology that caused such strife and war in the world for decades beginning in the very year, 1917, of the first apparition at Fatima. With the onset of communism in Russia, atheism replaced the country's ancient and revered religion of Christianity.

During the beginning of the twentieth century, state atheism, anti-clericalism, and religious persecution were implemented in Russia. Communists' use of violent force in attaining power led to millions of deaths. Therefore, it is not surprising that Our Lady strongly encouraged the consecration of Russia and prayer for her conversion. After Pope John Paul II consecrated the world to the Immaculate Heart of Mary in union with the bishops of the world, communism in Russia collapsed, and with it the monstrous doctrine of official state atheism in what was once a thoroughly Christian country and is becoming so again.

However, Our Lady's message was not only relevant for the time period during which it occurred. It is a message that remains relevant for us today. In fact, Pope John Paul II has told us that the message of

Fatima is even more relevant for us today than it was when it was first given to the visionaries by Our Lady in 1917.

Today, we are facing the greatest spiritual battle of our time. Radical secularism has become the new communism in our Western civilization. According to Father Gerard Beigel, "Secularism refers to a system of thought and belief which excludes God from human affairs. In short, secularism proclaims that the world we live in is all there is—there is no God, or if there is, He is too far beyond our understanding to be of any relevance to human life today." Secularism seeks to remove religion from the public square, to steal our religious freedoms, and to weaken the sanctity of human life by promoting abortion and attacking the basic tenets of Christian morality, particularly in regards to marriage and family life. In 1976, at the Eucharistic Congress in Philadelphia, Karol Woytola (the future Pope St. John Paul II) made a prophetic statement:

> We are now standing in the face of the greatest historical confrontation humanity has ever experienced. I do not think that the wide circle of the American Society, or the whole wide circle of the Christian Community realize this fully. We are now facing the final confrontation between the Church and the anti-church, between the gospel and the anti-gospel, between Christ and the antichrist. The confrontation lies within the plans of Divine Providence. It is, therefore, in God's Plan, and it must be a trial which the Church must take up, and face courageously.

So, then, despite the consecration of Russia and the fall of communism, world peace seems as elusive a goal as ever, and Western civilization has turned its back, for the most part, on its Christian heritage. The future pope was correct; the message of Fatima is more relevant today than ever, and Our Lady's call to live it in our daily lives remains. If we do, we have her assurance that she will shower us with the graces necessary for salvation at the hour of death, and there will be peace in the world.

Our Lady of Fatima . . . pray for us!

Appendix: Three Fatima Miracles

Hiroshima

At 2:45 a.m. on August 6, 1945, a B-29 bomber departed from the island of Tinian in the Pacific Ocean to drop the first atomic bomb on Japan. At 8:15 a.m. the bomb exploded eight city blocks away from the Jesuit church of Our Lady's Assumption in Hiroshima. A group of Jesuits were close to the epicenter of the attack on Hiroshima, but they survived the catastrophe, and the radiation that killed thousands in the following months had no effect on them. Experts were amazed that the priests had survived. The physicians who treated them after the disaster warned them that the radiation they received would produce serious lacerations, as well as disease and an early death. However, none of this happened.

One of them, a Father Hubert Schiffer later recalled that horrible day. According to Father Schiffer, having already celebrated Mass, he was about to eat breakfast, when there was a blinding flash of light followed by an incredible explosion. He was taken up and violently thrown about in the air—like a leaf in a gust of wind, he said. He would next open his

eyes on the ground, and, upon seeing the absolute devastation around him, was shocked to realize that, though wounded, he would survive. Perhaps even more miraculous than surviving the initial blast was the fact that none of the Jesuits suffered any after-effects from the radiation as was mentioned above. Father Schiffer himself, lived another thirty-three years and both wrote and spoke of his experiences at Hiroshima.

The religious fervently believed that they were protected by God and the Blessed Virgin Mary due to their devotion to the message of Fatima. They explained, "We were living the message of Fatima and we prayed the Rosary every day."

Pius XII

Pope Pius XII himself witnessed one of the most fascinating miracles following Fatima. In 1950, Pius XII witnessed the Miracle of the Sun four times. "A handwritten, unpublished note from Pope Pius XII" verified this information.

LA DOMENICA DEL CORRIERE

Supplemento settimanale illustrato del nuovo CORRIERE DELLA SERA - Abbonamenti: Italia, anno L. 1400, sem. L. 750 - Estero, anno L. 2000, sem. L. 1050

Anno 53 — N. 43   28 Ottobre 1951   L. 30.—

Una straordinaria visione del Papa. Il cardinale Tedeschini, legato pontificio alle celebrazioni del santuario di Fatima (Portogallo), ha narrato che nell'ottobre 1950 Pio XII, mentre passeggiava da solo nei giardini vaticani, vide per tre volte, sostenendone senza pena lo splendore, il sole trasformarsi in un disco d'argento e mettersi a ruotare su se stesso, proiettando in tutte le direzioni fasci di luce con colori cangianti: lo stesso meraviglioso fenomeno manifestatosi a varie persone parecchi anni fa, appunto nel paese di Fatima. (Disegno di Walter Molino)

On October 30, 1950, during his routine walk in the Vatican gardens, Pius XII reported, upon reaching the statue of Our Lady, being "awestruck by a phenomenon" that he had never seen before. He described it in the following way: "The sun, which was still quite high, looked like a pale, opaque sphere, entirely surrounded by a luminous circle." He was able to look at the sun "without the slightest bother. There was a very light little cloud in front of it."

In his note, he added, "The opaque sphere moved outward slightly, either spinning, or moving from left to right and vice versa. But within the sphere, you could see marked movements with total clarity and without interruption." He saw the phenomena on four separate occasions: "the 31st of October and Nov. 1, the day of the definition of the dogma of the Assumption, and then again Nov. 8, and after that, no more."

St. Pio of Pietrelcina

St. Pio of Pietrelcina, who is affectionately known as Padre Pio (1887–1968), was a young man of thirty living in Italy when the Fatima apparitions took place. One of the great mystics of the twentieth century, this well-known Capuchin priest had a strong devotion to the Blessed Virgin Mary. A man of poor health and much suffering, he was often misunderstood by his colleagues and other religious. Throughout his life, he promoted Marian devotion and encouraged others to pray the Rosary and to offer their sufferings to Jesus through Our Lady.

In April 1959, the pilgrim statue of the Immaculate Heart of Mary had come from Fatima to Italy by helicopter, stopping at the local capitals. Padre Pio, who was living at San Giovanni Rotundo, was unable to go to the places where the traveling Madonna appeared. He was ill with pleurisy, which made it impossible for him to even celebrate Mass,

but providentially, a schedule change was made and the holy man would be graced by a visit from his heavenly mother.

The statue was set to arrive on August 5, 1959. From his sickbed on July 27, Padre Pio announced the beginning of a novena, and he urged his flock to prepare for the arrival of the statue with renewed hearts. Every evening, he reminded them of the joy, the extraordinary blessing, and the special graces of this visit.

On the morning of August 6, he was finally able to make a brief visit to the church. He stopped in front of the statue of Our Lady to rest and he gave her a gold rosary. The statue was lowered before his face and he was able to kiss her. It was a gesture of great affection for his heavenly mother.

Between two and three in the afternoon on August 6, the helicopter carrying the pilgrim statue of Our Lady of Fatima headed for Sicily. From a window, Padre Pio watched the helicopter fly away with eyes filled with tears. He expressed great sorrow and disappointment at her departure.

Then, suddenly, Padre Pio felt a chill in his body and he began to shake. He quickly realized Our Lady cured him! He was stronger and healthier than he had ever been before in his life. He had experienced a complete healing. In thanksgiving, he sent a crucifix to Fatima in her honor.

Bibliography

Alonso, Joaquin M. "Sister Lucia: A Life of Sacrifice and Hope." *Soul* (Summer 2010): 12–13.

Apostoli, Andrew. *Fatima for Today: The Urgent Marian Message of Hope.* San Francisco: Ignatius Press, 2010.

Beigel, Gerard. "The Challenge of Secularism." *The California Mission* (November/December 1999). Accessed February 21, 2017. https://www.saint-mike.org/library/liberalism/challenge_secularism.html.

Benedict XVI. "Meeting with Young People of a Rehabilitation Community in the Church of the Sacred Heart, Sydney." EWTN. Accessed February 22, 2017. https://www.ewtn.com/library/papal-doc/b16wyd08rehab.htm.

Calloway, Donald H. *Champions of the Rosary.* Stockbridge, MA: Marian Press, 2016.

Carta, Paola. "Padre Pio and the Immaculate Heart of Mary." EWTN. Accessed February 16, 2017. https://www.ewtn.com/padrepio/mystic/Mary.htm.

"Chronology of the Three Seers." Shrine of Our Lady of the Rosary of Fatima. Accessed January 20, 2017. http://www.fatima.pt/en/pages/chronology-of-the-three-seers.

de Marchi, John. *The True Story of Fatima: A Complete Account of the Fatima Apparitions*. Self-Published, 2009.

de Montfort, Louis-Marie. *True Devotion to the Blessed Virgin Mary*. Bay Shore, NY: Montfort Publications, 1980.

de Oca, V. Montes. *More About Fatima and the Immaculate Heart of Mary*. L. Owen Traynor, 1979.

dos Santos, Lucia. *Fatima in Lucia's Own Words: Sister Lucia's Memoirs*, edited by Fr. Louis Kondor, SVD. Translated by Dominican Nuns of Perpetual Rosary. Postulation Centre, 1976.

Evert, Jason. *Saint John Paul the Great: His Five Loves*. Lakewood, CO: Totus Tuus Press and Lighthouse Catholic Media, 2014.

Fastiggi, Robert. "The Meaning of Fatima: 100 Years Later." *Our Sunday Visitor* (January 1–7, 2017).

"Fatima and the Popes." EWTN. http://www.ewtn.com/fatima/popes-and-fatima.asp.

"Fatima Shrine Receives Golden Rose." Zenit, published May 12, 2010. Accessed February 2, 2017. https://zenit.org/articles/fatima-shrine-receives-golden-rose/.

Flynn, Ted and Maureen, "Fatima the Cornerstone" in *The Thunder of Justice*. Herndon, VA: MaxKol Communications, 2010.

Foley, Donal Anthony. "May 13th, the Papacy and the Fatima Message."

World Apostolate of Fatima. Accessed February 3, 2017. https://wafusa.org/may-13th-the-papacy-and-the-fatima-message/.

Fournier, Keith A. "Feast of St. John Paul II, His Prophetic Warning to the U.S. Requires a Response," Catholic Online, published October 22, 2016. Accessed February 21, 2017. http://www.catholic.org/news/national/story.php?id=57376.

Haffert, John. *Her Own Words to the Nuclear Age.* Asbury, NJ: 101 Foundation, 1993.

Hardon, John. "The Essential Message of Fatima." The Real Presence Association. Accessed January 31, 2017. http://www.therealpresence.org/archives/Miracles/Miracles_007.htm.

———. "Pope Pius XII and Our Lady." The Real Presence Association. http://www.therealpresence.org/archives/Mariology/Mariology_005.htm.

John XXIII. *Journal of a Soul: The Autobiography of Pope John XXIII.* New York: Image, 1999.

John Paul II. *Gift and Mystery: On the Fiftieth Anniversary of My Priestly Ordination.* New York: Image, 1999.

———. "Message of Pope John Paul II to the Bishop of Coimbra on the Death of Sister Lucia." Libreria Editrice Vaticana, February 14, 2005. https://w2.vatican.va/content/john-paul-ii/en/letters/2005/documents/hf_jp-ii_let_20050214_bishop-coimbra.html.

———. "We Entrust, O Mary and Consecrate the Whole Word to Your Immaculate Heart!" EWTN. Accessed on January 31, 2017. http://www.ewtn.com/library/PAPALDOC/JPCONFAT.htm.

Mauriello, Matthew. "Our Lady and Pope Pius XII." In *Soul* 2 (2008): 18–19.

Miller, Michael. "Our Lady of Fatima and the Pilgrim Pope." *Lay Witness* (May/June 2007). Accessed January 31, 2017. http://www.cuf.org/2007/05/our-lady-of-fatima-and-the-pilgrim-pope/.

"The Miracle of Hiroshima – Jesuits survived the atomic bomb thanks to the rosary." Catholic News Agency, published August 9, 2015. http://www.catholicnewsagency.com/news/the-miracle-of-hiroshima-jesuits-survived-the-atomic-bomb-thanks-to-the-rosary-69261/.

Meissen, Randall J. "A Mother's Hand Guided the Bullets: John Paul II, Forgiving a Would-Be-Assassin." Catholic Online. Accessed February 3, 2017. http://www.catholic.org/news/saints/story.php?id=41174.

Nachef, Antoine. *Mary's Pope: John Paul II, Mary, and the Church Since Vatican II.* Franklin, WI: Sheed & Ward, 2000.

Our Lady of Fatima's Peace Plan from Heaven. Charlotte, NC: TAN Books, 1983.

"Padre Pio." World Apostolate of Fatima. Accessed on February 20, 2017. https://wafusa.org/padre-pio/.

"Papal Consecrations to the Blessed Virgin Mary: Pope Pius XII and Pope St. John Paul II." EWTN. Accessed January 31, 2017. http://www.ewtn.com/library/papaldoc/consecra.htm#JP2b.

Paul VI. *Marialis Cultus.* February 2, 1974. http://w2.vatican.va/content/paul-vi/en/apost_exhortations/documents/hf_p-vi_exh_19740202_marialis-cultus.html.

Pentin, Edward. "Pope Francis' Consecrating the World to Mary

Culminates Fatima Celebration." *National Catholic Register*, October 14, 2013.

"Pope's Message Read During Funeral of Sister Lucia." Catholic Online, published February 17, 2005. Accessed February 2, 2017. http://www.catholic.org/featured/headline.php?ID=1806.

Pronechen, Joseph. "Feting Fatima: How the Holy Fathers Have Feted Our Lady's Apparitions." National Catholic Register, January 8, 2017. http://www.ncregister.com/daily-news/feting-fatima-how-the-holy-fathers-have-honored-our-ladys-apparitions.

———. "Fatima for Today." National Catholic Register, April 29, 2011. Accessed February 21, 2017. http://www.ncregister.com/site/article/fatima-for-today.

Ratzinger, Joseph. "The Message of Fatima." Accessed January 16, 2017. http://www.vatican.va/roman_curia/congregations/cfaith/documents/rc_con_cfaith_doc_20000626_message-fatima_en.html.

Rinehart, Stephen and Richard F. Hubble. "Rosary Miracle - Safe in the Midst of Hiroshima Nuclear Blast !!" February 2000. http://www.holysouls.com/sar/rosarymiracle.htm.

Saunders, William P. "St. John Paul II and Mary." *The Arlington Catholic Herald,* May 13, 2015. Accessed January 29, 2017. http://catholicherald.com/Faith/Your_Faith/Straight_Answers/St__John_Paul_II_and_Mary/.

Schiffer, Hubert F., "The Rosary Of Hiroshima" (1953).Library Special Collections. Paper 2 http://digitalcommons.sacredheart.edu/library_specialcollections/2

Solimeo, Luiz Sergio. *Fatima: A Message More Urgent Than Ever*. Spring Grove, PA: American Society for the Defense of Tradition, Family, and Property, 2008.

"Stages of His Apostolic Trip to Portugal: Pope Benedict XVI." EWTN. Accessed February 2, 2017. http://www.ewtn.com/library/PAPALDOC/b16portstage.htm.

"Timeline." Marian Fathers of the Immaculate Conception of the B. V. M. Accessed February 1, 2017. http://www.marian.org/fatima/about/timeline.php.

Tindal-Robertson, Timothy. *Fatima, Russia and Pope John Paul II: How Mary Intervened to Deliver Russia from Marxist Atheism May 13, 1981-December 25, 1991*. Still River, MA: Ravengate Press, 1998.

About the Author

JEAN M. HEIMANN is a Catholic author and freelance writer with an M.A. in Theology, a parish minister and speaker, a psychologist and educator, and an Oblate with the Community of St. John. She is a member of the Blue Army and the founder of the Our Lady of Fatima Rosary and Study group. Jean is the author of *Seven Saints for Seven Virtues* (Servant, 2014) and *Learning to Love with the Saints: A Spiritual Memoir* (Mercy, 2016). Visit Jean at her website www.jeanmheimann.com through which you can also access her award-winning blog, Catholic Fire.

Image Credits

Front Cover, P iv–v Our Lady of Fatima statue, Fatima, Portugal/ Francisco Seco/ AP Images

Back Cover Fatima Sanctuary / ramosnuno / iStock

P i Fatima pilgrims' Virgin statue (photo) / Godong/UIG / Bridgeman Images

P viii Pilgrims walk on their knees at Fatima Sanctuary, in Fatima, Portugal, on Wednesday, May 12, 2010. Pope Benedict XVI will visit the sanctuary to celebrate the 10th anniversary of the beatification of Francisco and Jacinta Marto. © PAULO AMORIM/AE/AE (Agencia Estado via AP Images)

P xv Pope Francis with the statue of Our Lady of Fatima Pope Francis celebrates mass with the statue of Our Lady of Fatima, Vatican City, Rome, Italy - 13 Oct 2013 © Rex Features via AP Images

P xvi–xvii The Sanctuary of Fatima, which is also referred to as the Basilica of Our Lady of Fatima, Portugal © saiko3p, Shutterstock

P xiii Fatima, Portugal / phbcz / iStock

P xxii A sculpture depicting the three little shepherds Giacinta Marto, Francisco Marto e Lucia dos Santos praying is placed in the holy place of Our Lady of Fatima 1984. © Mondadori Portfolio/ Angelo Cozzi / Bridgeman Images

P 3 Why Seek Ye the Living Among the Dead?, 1905 (oil on canvas), Pyle, Howard (1853-1911) / American Illustrators Gallery, NYC / www.asap-worldwide.com / Bridgeman Images

P 4 Lucia dos Santos and her cousins Francisco and Jacinta Marto in 1917 in Fatima in Portugal where Virgin Mary appeared many times / Photo © Tallandier / Bridgeman Images

P 8 The three children of Fátima: Lúcia Santos (age 10, pictured in the middle) and her two cousins: Francisco (age 9) and Jacinta Marto (age 7) holding their rosaries. Public domain via Wikimedia Commons

P 9 A woman praying in Fatima shrine © Mondadori Portfolio/Archivio Angelo Cozzi/Angelo Cozzi / Bridgeman Images

P 10 Our Lady of Fatima, Charles Bousseron Chambers, Restored Traditions

P 13 Images of Our Lady of Fatima with Shepherd Children © Antonio Jorge Nunes, Shutterstock

P 16–17 The Annunciation, 1651-52 (oil on canvas), Poerson, Charles (1609-67) / Musee des Beaux-Arts, Arras, France / Bridgeman Images

P 19 Our Lady of Grace, Charles Bousseron Chambers, Restored Traditions

P 21 Portuguese women praying, Fatima, Portugal / Mondadori Portfolio/Sergio del Grande / Bridgeman Images

P 23 The Virgin and Child with St. Dominic (oil on canvas), Flemish School / Sint-Hermes Kerk, Ronse, Belgium / Photo © Paul Maeyaert / Bridgeman Images

P 24 Allegory of the Battle of Lepanto, 7th October 1571 (oil on canvas), Veronese, (Paolo Caliari) (1528-88) / Galleria dell' Accademia, Venice, Italy / Bridgeman Images

P 26 Hell (oil on panel), Bouts, Dirck (c.1415-75) / Musee des Beaux-Arts, Lille, France / Bridgeman Images

P 28–29 The Last Judgement (oil on canvas), Meyer, Conrad (1618-89) / Private Collection / Photo © Bonhams, London, UK / Bridgeman Images

P 32 Paradise Lost, 1867 (oil on canvas), Cabanel, Alexandre (1823-89) / Private Collection / Photo © Christie's Images / Bridgeman Images

P 35 Crucifixion group on Milsenburg mountain at Rhoen landscape, Germany 1930s (b/w photo) / United Archives/Lämmel / Bridgeman Images

P 36–37 Cross over Gorner Glacier, Switzerland © Byunau Konstantin, Shutterstock

P 39 The Conversion of St. Paul, 1767 (oil on canvas), Lepicie, Nicolas-Bernard (1735-84) / Private Collection / © John Mitchell Fine Paintings / Bridgeman Images

P 40–41 Worshippers pray and walk on their knees to the Our Lady of Fatima shrine, in Fatima, centre Portugal, Tuesday, May 13, 2014. (AP Photo/ Francisco Seco)

P 43 Oswiecim, 1979. Pope John Paul II's first Pilgrimage to Poland. / Forum / Bridgeman Images

P 44 Bialystok airport, 05.06.1991. Pope John Paul II's 4th Pilgrimage to Poland. / Forum / Bridgeman Images

P 46–47 L'Osservatorio Romano

P 49 Revolutionary sailors in a church in Lisbon, 1910 (b/w photo) / © SZ Photo / Scherl / Bridgeman Images

P 50 Our Lady of the Rosary, Charles Bousseron Chambers, Restored Traditions

P 53 Capelinha das Aparições de Fátima, Public Domain, Wikimedia Commons

P 55 Basilica of Our Lady of the Rosary in Fatima on a sunny day – Portugal, © Vadim Petrakov, Shutterstock

P 56 Miracle of the sun, Fatima, 13th October 1917 (b/w photo), French Photographer, (20th century) / Private Collection / Archives Charmet / Bridgeman Images

P 57 Our Lady of Mount Carmel (oil on canvas), Wappers, Gustave or Gustaaf (1803-74) / Church of St. Charles Borromeo, Antwerp, Belgium / Bridgeman Images

P 59 A photostatic copy of a page from Ilustração Portuguesa, October 29, 1917, showing the crowd looking at the "miracle of the sun" (attributed to the Virgin Mary). Public Domain, Wikimedia Commons

P 60 Francisco and Jacinta Marto in 1917 in Fatima in Portugal where Virgin Mary appeared many times / Photo © Tallandier / Bridgeman Images

P 62 Francisco Marto of Fatima / Photo © CCI / Bridgeman Images

P 63 Jacinta Marto of Fatima / Photo © CCI / Bridgeman Images

P 65 Our Lady of the Immaculate Heart, Charles Bousseron Chambers, Restored Traditions

P 68 Jacinta Marto, Lucia dos Santos, Public Domain, Wikimedia Commons

P 71 Lucia dos Santos (1907-2005), one of the three children who see the apparition of Virgin Mary in 1917 in Fatima in Portugal, here as a nun, c. 1930 / Photo © Tallandier / Bridgeman Images

P 73 The Madonna of the Rosary, 1670-80 (oil on canvas), Murillo, Bartolome Esteban (1618-82) / Dulwich Picture Gallery, London, UK / Bridgeman Images

P 75 The Trinity (oil on canvas), Tintoretto, Jacopo Robusti (1518-94) / Galleria Sabauda, Turin, Italy / Bridgeman Images

P 77 Rome, Italy - June 2015 - Adoration monstrance with the Blessed Sacrament © Thoom, Shutterstock

P 78 Santuario Guadalupe Rianxo Galicia, Public Domain, Wikimedia Commons

P 82–83 Aurora Borealis, visible in autumn 2003 over Bayreuth, Bavaria, Germany © Jens Mayer, Shutterstock

P 84 L'Osservatorio Romano

P 85 Pie XI / Photo © Spaarnestad / Bridgeman Images

P 86 Pope Pius XI, 1931 (b/w photo) / © SZ Photo / Scherl / Bridgeman Images

P 87 One of the first pictures of Pope Pius XII after his coronation, Rome, 1939 (b/w photo) / Private Collection / Bridgeman Images

P 89 Pope Pius XII (Eugenio Pacelli, pope in 1939-1958) with crowd after the bombings in Rome august 14, 1943 during WW2, Pie XII / Photo © Spaarnestad / Bridgeman Images

P 90 Pope-elect John XXIII before his elevation, 1958 / J. T. Vintage / Bridgeman Images

P 91 Pope John XXIII, Ange Joseph Roncalli (1881-1963, pontificate 1958-1963) during visit of Loreto shrine on october 7, 1962 / Bridgeman Images

P 92 Pope Paul VI (Giovanni Battista Montini, pope in 1963-1978) during Eucharistic congress in Pisa june 13, 1965, Paul VI / Bridgeman Images

P 93 Pope Paul VI holds the hand Sister Lucia Marto as they stand at the base of the statue of Our Lady of Fatima in the Basilica at Fatima, Portugal in this May 13, 1967 file photo. (AP Photo)

P 95 1983 - Portrait of Pope John Paul II. / Forum / Bridgeman Images

P 96 Photo shows Pope John Paul II donating a rosary to the statue of Virgin Mary at the Chapel of the Apparitions in Fatima, May 12, 1982, in Fatima. The Pontiff came here to thank the Holy Virgin to have saved his life one year ago in an attempt on his life in Rome, Italy. (AP-PHOTO)

P 98 Scene in St. Peters Square on May 13. 1981, when Pope John Paul II was shot. A gun can be seen at far left above the head of a man wearing sunglasses (AP Photo)

P 101 Pope John Paul II, Papal Assissination Attempt, Hulton Archive, Photographer: Keystone, Getty Images

P 102 Photo taken on May 13, 1991 from Sister Lucy with Pope John Paul II in Fatima (center of Portugal). Last survivor of the three small shepherds who have reported appearances of the Virgin Mary in Fatima. Photo: JOAO PAULO TRINDADE / AFP, Getty Images

P 104 Pope Benedict XVI smiles to faithful gathered at Fatima's Sanctuary, Wednesday, May 12, 2010 at a candle light vigil. (AP Photo/Gregorio Borgia)

P 105 Pope Benedict XVI prays in front of the statue of the Virgin Mary at Fatima's Sanctuary, Wednesday, May 12 2010. (AP Photo/Gregorio Borgia)

P 106–107 Pope Benedict XVI rides on the Popemobile as he leaves Fatima's Sanctuary, Wednesday, May 12, 2010 during a candle light vigil. (AP Photo/ Emilio Morenatti)

P 109 Pope Francis, Vatican City, Vatican City State / Mondadori Portfolio/ Archivio Grzegorz Galazka/Grzegorz Galazka / Bridgeman Images

P 110 The Fatima Shrine statue, ferried by a helicopter, Rome Saturday, May 13, 2006. The statue, with one of the bullets which struck Pope John Paul II embedded in it as a memento, joined a procession toward St. Peter's square where exactly 25 years earlier a Turkish gunman shot and gravely wounded the late pontiff. Pope John Paul II has credited his survival of the May 13, 1981, assassination attempt to the intercession of the Madonna di Fatima. In background is St. Peter's Basilica. (AP Photo/Pier Paolo Cito)

P 111 Pope Francis pays homage to the statue of Our Lady of Fatima during his weekly general audience in St. Peter's Square at the Vatican, Wednesday, May 13, 2015. (L'Osservatore Romano/Pool Photo via AP)

P 112 Our Lady of Fatima Shrine statue is carried in procession prior to the start of a Mass celebrated by Pope Francis. Oct. 13, 2013. (AP Photo/Riccardo De Luca)

P 114 Immaculate Heart of Mary, Godong/ UIG / Bridgeman Images

P 115 Germany / Russia / Soviet Union: Red Army soldiers raising the Soviet flag atop the Brandenburg Gate, Berlin, 1945 / Pictures from History / Bridgeman Images

P 116–117 The Square of the Sanctuary of Fatima full of pilgrims, Portugal, 1967 (photo) / Mondadori Portfolio/Sergio del Grande / Bridgeman Images

P 118 Worshippers pray during a candle light vigil at the Our Lady of Fatima shrine, in Fatima, central Portugal, Tuesday, May 12, 2015. (AP Photo/ Francisco Seco)

P 120 A statue of Our Lady of Fatima is carried during a candle light vigil at the Our Lady of Fatima shrine, in Fatima, central Portugal, Tuesday, May 12, 2015. (AP Photo/Francisco Seco)

P 122 Hiroshima in ruins, Japan, 1945 (b/w photo) / © Galerie Bilderwelt / Bridgeman Images

P 123 Una straordinaria visione del Papa (colour litho), Molino, Walter (1915-1997) / Private Collection / © Look and Learn / Bridgeman Images

P 125 Attendance at the Mass of Rev. Pius Francis Pio, O.F.M., Cap. (above), who has been a stigmatic for 39 years, the longest recorded in the history of stigmatics, will highlight the Blue Army Pilgrimage, it was revealed today by Rt. Rev. Harold V. Colgan, founder and international director of the Blue Army of Our Lady of Fatima, at its national headquarters in Washington, D.C., June 4, 1956. (AP Photo)

P 134 Night photograph of the Sanctuary of Fatima, altar of the Catholic word. Portugal. © cineuno, Shutterstock